Praise for
Help! I'm Married to an Intercessor

Lovingly and with humor, Eddie Smith opens the prayer closet door to show the blessings and challenges of being an intercessor—or those who live with them. This book is filled with wisdom and great insight into a lifestyle of prayer.

Elizabeth Alves
Author of *Becoming a Prayer Warrior*
President, Intercessors International, Inc.
Bulverde, Texas

Full of down-to-earth, refreshing pearls of godly wisdom, this book is a must for the spouse of anyone with a special calling of God.

Bill and Vonette Bright
Cofounders, Campus Crusade for Christ
Orlando, Florida

What a wonderful problem to face! There's a nation overflowing with followers of Christ who have been called to the ministry of intercession, and they are having vital impact on our generation. So, it's about time someone helped us figure out how to live with them—because we sure can't live without them! Serving with me on America's National Prayer Committee, Eddie has demonstrated a godly wisdom about prayer that comes through this guide loud and clear. It's a book that's been begging to be written!

David Bryant
Founder and President, Concerts of Prayer International
New Providence, N

Moving from the humorous to the hazardous, Eddie Smith presents a balanced, instructive look at the prayer life of an intercessor. Speaking from years of firsthand experience, the author has a message to benefit the personal devotional life of any Christian couple.

Sandra G. Clopine
Coordinator, National Prayer Center of the Assemblies of God
Springfield, Missouri

Eddie Smith has blended accounts of his personal ministry experiences with lessons learned from his intercessor wife, then added a measure of divine revelation to produce a delightfully written book sure to help all those who work with or live with intercessors. If you're into prayer—and especially if you're not—read this book!

Dan R. Crawford
Professor of Evangelism and Spiritual Formation and
Chair of Prayer
Southwestern Baptist Theological Seminary
Fort Worth, Texas

Help! I'm Married to an Intercessor is chock-full of valuable insights not found anywhere else. Eddie Smith has tackled a cutting-edge topic, one that when understood by the Church will yield a profound harvest for the Kingdom.

Jonathan Graf
Editor, *Pray!* Magazine
Colorado Springs, Colorado

Eddie Smith writes with the wisdom of Solomon and the humor of Will Rogers! *Help! I'm Married to an Intercessor* is a primer for the uninitiated and a valuable, encouraging tool for the seasoned intercessor.

Ted Haggard
Senior Pastor, New Life Church
Colorado Springs, Colorado

Like an artist with a pen instead of a brush, the movement of the author's pen is akin to the artist who paints in oils. The movement from the old to the new; from the great to the small; from the personal experience and to the written word; from teaching us how to get started to how to get the job done. And most important of all, Eddie Smith conveys his love for and dedication to God's Holy Spirit without sending into the background our Lord Jesus Christ.

This book is a must for people who want to see a revival in our day. Eddie Smith deals with the most important responsibility in the Christian world—communication and communing with the Creator of the universe—with such an easy flow of words, every preacher, every Sunday School teacher, every church worker should read it.

Rudy A. Hernandez
International Evangelist
Grand Prairie, Texas

Eddie Smith writes with warmth, humor and transparency. God's wisdom pours out of the author's heart and onto these pages to instruct, inform and inspire us.

Tim James
Co-coordinator, U.S. Prayer Track
President, Truth International Ministries
Houston, Texas

Help! I'm Married to an Intercessor is a rare combination of hilarious humor, practical instruction and superb inspiration. It's an easy read, yet laden with great truths. Any Christian who believes in prayer and yearns to practice it more faithfully will profit greatly from this book. I recommend it highly.

Larry L. Lewis
National Facilitator for Celebrate Jesus 2000
Mission America
Lilburn, Georgia

A strong vein of practical instruction and godly wisdom runs throughout this work on intercession. While promoting healthy relationships is central to this book, affirmation of intercessors and clear guidance in the work of intercession abound. Pastors, as well as spouses, will be richly aided in their relationships and ministry with those called to intercession. Thank you, Eddie, for the encouragement and correction you have given us in your book!

Steve Meeks
Senior Pastor, Calvary Community Church
Houston, Texas

Intercessory prayer is essential to the kingdom work of Christ, to great local churches, to healthy families and to our lives as Christians. Yet the ministry of intercession is little understood and greatly underappreciated! Every pastor, every Christian leader and yes, every believer needs to read *Help! I'm Married to an Intercessor*. Eddie delightfully weaves truths about intercession with humor and captivating human interest stories that help the reader understand and appreciate these unsung heroes of the faith.

Darrell W. Robinson
Special Assistant for Evangelism
North American Mission Board
Mobile, Alabama

Eddie Smith uses his wonderful sense of humor to skillfully define the ministry of intercession. God has entrusted him with a "box seat" at the drama of a life totally consecrated to go beyond the veil and seek the face of Jesus. It is my prayer that the beautiful relationship between Eddie and Alice Smith will serve to encourage others to empower their spouses to become all that God has called them to be at the place of prayer.

Mary Lance V. Sisk
Chairperson, Love Your Neighbor as Yourself
National Committee USA
A.D. 2000 North American Women's Track
Charlotte, North Carolina

A one-of-a-kind book! Eddie Smith has helped me to understand intercessors and their ministry in a whole new way. This electrifying book will send positive shock waves throughout the whole Body of Christ!

C. Peter Wagner
Cofounder, World Prayer Center
Colorado Springs, Colorado

Beware! This book is dangerous, contagious and awfully fun to read. Going through it, you may become a "prayer nut" and secretly wish your spouse would one day become an intercessor. You may even end up spending several hours a day in a prayer closet! But this book *will* bring you closer to the heart of God and make you a blessing to countless peoples around the world. Read it!

Thomas Wang
International Chairman, A.D. 2000 & Beyond Movement
Argyle, Texas

Help! I'm Married to an Intercessor

EDDIE SMITH

Renew

A Division of Gospel Light
Ventura, California, U.S.A.

Published by Renew Books
A Division of Gospel Light
Ventura, California, U.S.A.
Printed in U.S.A.

Renew Books is a ministry of Gospel Light, an evangelical Christian publisher dedicated to serving the local church. We believe God's vision for Gospel Light is to provide church leaders with biblical, user-friendly materials that will help them evangelize, disciple and minister to children, youth and families.

It is our prayer that this Renew book will help you discover biblical truth for your own life and help you meet the needs of others. May God richly bless you.

For a free catalog of resources from Renew Books and Gospel Light please call your Christian supplier, or contact us at 1-800-4-GOSPEL or at www.gospellight.com.

Cover Design by Barbara LeVan Fisher
Interior Design by Mario Ricketts
Edited by David Webb

Library of Congress Cataloging-in-Publication Data
Smith, Eddie.
    Help! I'm married to an intercessor / Dutch Sheets.
        p.   cm.
    Includes bibliographical references.
    ISBN 0-8307-2200-9 (trade paper)
    1. Intercessory prayer—Christianity.   2. Spouses—Religious life.
    3. Smith, Alice, 1950–   4. Smith, Eddie. I. Title.
    BV210.2.S627   1998
    248.3'2—dc21   98-38023
                                                                    CIP

1 2 3 4 5 6 7 8 9 10 11 12 13 14 15 16 17 18 19 20 / 04 03 02 01 00 99 98

Rights for publishing this book in other languages are contracted by Gospel Literature International (GLINT). GLINT also provides technical help for the adaptation, translation and publishing of Bible study resources and books in scores of languages worldwide. For further information, write to GLINT at P.O. Box 4060, Ontario, CA 91761-1003, U.S.A. You may also send e-mail to Glintint@aol.com, or visit their web site at www.glint.org.

This book
is dedicated to God's wonderful intercessors.
With your faithfulness in prayer,
we will see the glory of God.

Contents

Foreword

Prayer changes things! The Word of God is very clear about this and every believer believes it. And yet, there is much confusion about how to pray, when to pray and where to pray.

Eddie and Alice Smith are both powerful prayer warriors, though Alice is "officially" the intercessor. I have prayed with them and been prayed for by them, and I have been significantly impacted by both experiences. What I know about this couple is that they are no strangers to the presence of God. They commune with Him on a consistent, ongoing basis.

Help! I'm Married to an Intercessor will speak into the life of any man or woman married to an intercessor. I chuckled aloud as I read Eddie's candid account of being married to a woman who is not only an extraordinary prayer warrior, but a gifted speaker and author as well. This book will minister wisdom and understanding to those of you who find yourselves in similar circumstances.

But the book is much more than that. This is a "how to" book on prayer by a man who knows the power of prayer. *Help! I'm Married to an Intercessor* is full of wisdom, knowledge, exhortation and challenges that, if heeded, will draw every reader into closer communion with the Father. I can't think of any place I'd rather be, can you?

Terry Meeuwsen
Cohost, "The 700 Club"

Foreword

Several Hebrew and Greek phrases from the Old and New Testaments are used to define for us the term *intercession*. These phrases carry such meanings as *hit the mark, pressure, influence, to light upon, to lay a burden upon* and, of course, *to intercede*. My favorite of these is *to light upon*. It connotes coming upon something accidentally, yet when you are there, you realize it is a divine appointment. It is this sense you will have as you begin to read the book you now hold in your hands.

Eddie Smith is married to a truly wonderful woman—a wonderful woman who just happens to be an intercessor. Eddie's insights, gleaned from years of firsthand experience as the husband of a gifted prayer warrior, are invaluable for those of us who would learn more about a lifestyle of prayer.

I believe that while the whole Church is called to the ministry of intercession, there are indeed those who are called to bear a significant measure of responsibility in this area. Boaz told his servants to take a special concern for Ruth, who was gleaning in the fields, and he ordered them to "let fall also some of the handfuls of purpose for her" (Ruth 2:16, *KJV*). Eddie Smith has gleaned some remarkable principles of intercession from his marriage to Alice.

This book could easily have been titled *Help! I Pastor Intercessors.* I have had many conversations with pastors who struggle with the tensions between the ministry of intercession and other aspects of church life. Like Job, their cry was "If only there were someone to arbitrate between us, to lay his hand upon us both" (Job 9:33). In this book, Eddie Smith functions graciously as the arbitrator who lays his hand upon both the intercessor and the other. As a pastor and husband, he knows both worlds. The Father has allowed some "handfuls of purpose" to fall to him, and he shares that wisdom with us in a book that will become the tool that intercessors and those who relate to them can utilize as a means for understanding one another.

While Alice Smith's commitment to prayer is radically different from her husband's, what is evident in these pages is the life of prayer the author himself has learned to live and to teach. Eddie Smith's *Help! I'm Married to an Intercessor* is ultimately a guide to the basic principles of intercession. It could easily become a primer on prayer that causes the Body of Christ to say, "Aha! This is it!"

Joseph L. Garlington
Senior Pastor
Covenant Church of Pittsburgh

Acknowledgments

I thank . . .

. . . my parents, Robert and Marguerite Smith, who have invested their very lives in the lives of others for Christ's sake. You have been faithful to God and to me. Thank you for your examples in prayer.

. . . my wife, Alice, who is my personal intercessor. Thank you, Sweetheart, for becoming so vulnerable and so transparent within these pages. Thank you for the tireless way you model and mentor others in intercession. And thank you for your help in preparing this manuscript!

. . . our children, Robert, Julia, Bryan and Ashlee. You are the joy of our hearts!

. . . our U.S. Prayer Track Board Members.

. . . Houston House of Prayer and Calvary Community Church in Houston, Texas.

. . . our personal intercessors past, who invested their hearts and lives in prayer for us.

. . . our current intercessors:

Janet Adams, Houston, TX

Glen & Dianne Becker, Houston, TX

Pamela & Gary Bettis, Bedford, TX

Steven & Nancy Burke, Cypress, TX

Jeff & Mary Kay Chapman, Houston, TX

Kathie Chan, Houston, TX

Peter & JoAnn Crowson, Live Oak, CA

Marti & Hugh Davidson, Houston, TX

John & Nancy Day, Waco, TX (Alice's brother and his wife)

Martha Day, Lake Jackson, TX (Alice's mother)

Charles Doolittle, Camarillo, CA

Bob & Betty Dorsett, Elgin, TX

Bill & Connie Fisher, Cypress, TX

Wayne & Janice Friery, Houston, TX
Linda Fulmer, Lindale, TX
Greg & Becca Greenwood, Katy, TX
Jack & Pam Greenwood, Gulfport, MS
Linda & Jeff Hanawalt, Houston, TX
Jean Harless, Buhl, AL
Bill Harrell, Houston, TX
Pam Holecheck, Colorado Springs, CO
Brenda Kidd, Houston, TX
Tim & Joyce James, Houston, TX
Necole Jones, Upper Marlboro, MD
Mark & Renita LeCrone, Houston, TX
Eraina & Skeeter Lothringer, Cypress, TX
Anne Money, Houston, TX
Matt & Sally Montgomery, Spring, TX
Mark & Becky Nazarenus, Fishers, IN
Grace Pieper, St. Louis, MO
Chuck Pierce, Colorado Springs, CO
Jane Rhodes, Houston, TX
Lydia Ripley, Houston, TX
Nancy Robinson, McAllen, TX
Neal & Darla Ryden, Houston, TX
Bill Shobe, Washington, DC
Jettie Stanley, Silsbie, TX
Debbie Walker, Houston, TX
Robin & Dan White, Houston, TX
Sue White, San Antonio, TX
Megan Yarbrough, Houston, TX
Steven & Maija Yoes, Pasadena, CA
Doug Fletcher, San Antonio, TX
Gene Hunter, Plano, TX
Robert & Sue Smith (my parents)
Robert Smith (our oldest son)
John & Ardelle Dame, Cypress, TX
Peter & Doris Wagner, Colorado Springs, CO
Richard Cottrell, Houston, TX
Mrs. Mickie Winborn, Houston, TX
Rev. Michael Cave, Houston, TX

Introduction

To the Spouse of an Intercessor:

This book is written largely for men and women who are married to praying people, or intercessors. Intercessors are people who approach prayer as a ministry on behalf of other people or causes. Being married to a gifted intercessor is not unlike being married to a pastor, a missionary or any other minister.

Intercessors are front-line troops in the ancient war between God and Satan. If you are married to an intercessor, this makes your spouse a warrior—and a spiritual target. It takes a remarkable person to fulfill the position of intercessor and assume the awesome tasks thereof. You've probably also discovered that the role of the intercessor can also require a great deal from the people who live with them.

As you are reading about my wife, Alice, and our experiences, perhaps you will be able to relate. Maybe the insights herein will confirm your own experiences, possibly even reassure you. Many of you could no doubt write your own books.

As the spouse of an intercessor, you may already know this role offers you a unique opportunity for Kingdom partnership. Frankly, as the husband of an intercessor and having been the pastor of many, I don't feel there is any more important ministry today than the ministry of intercession. God has His hand on intercession and intercessors today as never before!

My friend Skeeter is an award-winning bass angler. He and Eraina, his beautiful wife, own a successful automobile repair business. He is an outdoorsman, a man's man. Skeeter and I are in the same boat. He is also married to an intercessor. When God speaks to Eraina, she hears Him. Countless times she has shared with us secret things the Lord has told her about us. Most of what she has relayed to us has come to pass.

One night we had a meeting of intercessors in our home. Noted author C. Peter Wagner and Doris, his wife and administrator, were our guests. Pete was answering questions and discussing the ministry of intercessory prayer.

At one point, Skeeter interjected humorously, "I have to be a faithful husband. If I ever cheated on Eraina, before I could get home God would already have told her who it was, where we went and what we did! God tells my wife everything!"

We all laughed, but I seriously asked Peter, who was then writing a series of books about prayer, "When are you going to write a book to help those of us who are married to intercessors?"

Agreeing that it needed to be done, he smiled and suggested, "You're married to one. You write it!"

God has rewards in heaven for His faithful intercessors. He also has rewards for those of you who make this important ministry possible. As you read this book, may you be blessed and challenged to understand, support and love your spouse even more.

To the Intercessor:

This is a description of the relationship Alice and I enjoy. Please understand that other husbands and wives with different personalities, spiritual gifts, goals and convictions will experience marriage differently.

It is important then that, as you read this book, you seek to impose neither these, nor your own ideas on your spouse. Receive your spouse as a gift from God to you and serve him or her faithfully.

The apostle Peter writes to husbands that they are to "dwell with [their wives] according to knowledge" (1 Pet. 3:7, *KJV*). This is true of every successful relationship. The only way to know each other is through open communication. Keep the lines of communication open in your marriage. Seek to understand your spouse's point of view, what he or she expects of you, and work accordingly with your partner. God promises in the same passage that, in doing so, your prayers will not be hindered.

Eddie Smith

1

She's Crazy About You, Jesus!

One morning my wife, Alice, went shopping for building supplies for a project I was working on. Being an intercessor and not a construction worker, she was largely unfamiliar with these items and spent a considerable amount of time in the hardware store looking for them.

Alice was finally standing in the checkout line when, suddenly, she had a brief vision. In her mind's eye—a closed vision—she saw a man standing in my office pointing a gun at me.

Immediately she grabbed her purse, abandoned her cart with the items she had worked so hard to find, and ran to the car. Alice began to intercede, even as she drove home. Once home, she rushed inside to her prayer closet, where she began crying out to the Lord.

She has since been asked, "Alice, why didn't you call the office and ask if he was alright?"

"It was time to pray, not take a survey," she replies.

Alice prayed for 45 minutes until the burden and the sense of urgency subsided. Only then did she call the office and ask, "Eddie, are you okay?"

"Yeah, fine." I answered. "Why do you ask?"

She told me about her vision and how she had entered into prayer.

"Oh that," I explained. "He just got saved."

That morning I had had a counseling session with a medical doctor who was in ill health, separated from his wife, addicted to narcotics and suicidal. After I led him to Christ—and through some significant deliverance—he explained how he had loaded a pistol that morning and placed it on his kitchen counter, intending to bring it to my office and first kill me, then himself. For some "unexplained reason," he absentmindedly left the pistol on the kitchen counter.

Yes, being married to an intercessor definitely has its advantages! But I'm getting ahead of myself. As famed radio commentator Paul Harvey would say, "And now . . . the rest of the story."

How I Found a Virtuous Woman

> Who can find a virtuous woman? For her price is far above rubies. The heart of her husband doth safely trust in her, so that he shall have no need of spoil. She will do him good and not evil all the days of her life (Prov. 31:10-12, *KJV*).

The summer of 1970 was a lonely time for me, living in motels, moving from town to town, city to city as a single, itinerant evangelist in my twenties. Every night when the revival services concluded, I was off to a late-night meal and then to a lonely motel room.

Because of my travel schedule, I rarely spent time at my small apartment in South Houston. For the most part, it was only a place to hang my clothes and stash boxes of my unsold record albums. It, too, was a lonely spot.

The Encounter

Walking into the old auditorium of First Baptist Church that Sunday night, then located in downtown Houston, little did I know how my life was about to be changed. I was there to sing for a citywide youth rally, where I would be sharing the stage with a sharp contemporary Christian singing group from Houston Baptist University called Implosion. They were directed by Pete Sanchez, who would later write the classic worship chorus "I Exalt Thee" and appear on several Hosanna Integrity worship albums.

As the former director of The Spurrlows, a nationally known contemporary musical group at the time, I immediately found myself interested in Implosion's work from a technical standpoint. Impressed by their sharp visual presentation and tight vocal harmonies, I was really into the concert. That is, until I caught sight of Pete's lead soprano—a slight, cute blonde with a magnificent voice. The rest of the evening, my thoughts were only about her.

Following the service, I stopped a member of the group to ask about her and whether she was married. He assured me that Alice Day wasn't married, although she had several admirers waiting in the wings.

Mentally unplugging for the evening, I took refuge in my usual late-night burger and milkshake and made my way to the lonely solitude of my South Houston apartment. (To this day my heart goes out to singles. To remain single requires a grace gift from the Lord!)

An Unexpected Bonus!

On the schedule for the following night was ministry at Freddie Gage's Pulpit in the Shadows, a street ministry designed to reach out to drug addicts and to the homeless. Parking my car near Pulpit in the Shadows and locking all the doors, I worked my way through an odorous crowd of hippies and winos to get inside the run-down, white-framed, abandoned church building. Body odors mixed with the pungent, acrid smell of marijuana smoke was almost stifling.

My ears pricked up when I heard the familiar sounds of musicians warming up and instruments being tuned. Suddenly, my heart did a back flip! There vocalizing on stage was the same beautiful, blonde soprano. Immediately I knew that this week was going to be different!

After the service, everyone was challenged to pair up and go into the streets to witness for Christ. Here was my chance! Fighting my way through the crowd to the place where Alice Day was standing, I introduced myself to her. I handed her a stack of gospel tracts and invited her to go out witnessing with me.

She declined. My heart sank, but I wouldn't be deterred. So I asked, "Can we go for coffee when this is over?"

Again, she declined. Disappointed, I left solo.

If at First You Don't Succeed . . .

On Tuesday, the second night of the three-day meeting, I approached Alice again with the same offer at the close of the service. This time she agreed to go. We went together into the streets of downtown Houston, passing out tracts, sharing the gospel message and praying for the people. The power of prayer was evident that night, as several people trusted Christ as their Savior. It was an awesome evening! God blended our gifts and skills together in a powerful way.

Now I had been a soul winner since elementary school, faithfully sharing my faith through high school, the Navy and college. During the late 1960s, at the height of the hippie revolution, I had worked two years on Hollywood's Sunset Strip with noted California evangelist Arthur Blessitt. We witnessed in bars, nightclubs, strip joints, psychedelic "trip" rooms, X-rated movie theaters and biker hangouts.

With the exception of my own mother, a faithful and strong witness, I had never met a woman as bold as Alice. This woman was fearless! She witnessed to everything that moved. And if it didn't move, she stuck a gospel tract on it!

There was something special about her. She possessed an intense passion for the Lord and compassion for the lost. Prayer was important to her—more important to her than it was to me and to most other Christians I had known. That night she shared with me about her life and her call to the ministry. Once more I invited her to go with me to get something to eat. Again, she declined!

And I Thought I Didn't Have a Prayer . . .

Arriving early Wednesday night, I waited impatiently until time for us to hit the streets again. Alice agreed to join me once more and we were off! The experience was even more dynamic than the night before. God's Holy Spirit was on us! The effect of our ministry together was simply greater than the sum of its parts. It was obvious to me that God was doing something special!

Later that night when we returned to Pulpit in the Shadows, again I suggested that we go out for coffee. Again she refused.

"Alice, you need to get to know me," I blurted out presumptuously. "I'm going to marry you!" Why I said that I cannot explain.

Obviously jolted by my statement, yet eminently unflappable, she bravely smiled and said, "Okay, let's go eat."

J. Vernon McGee, the late teacher and host of "Through the Bible," once said on his radio program, "I asked my wife to marry me on our second date. I waited till then because I didn't want her to think I was in a hurry."

The next six weeks were like a whirlwind as I traveled the eastern seaboard ministering in citywide evangelistic crusades. Every night from my hotel room, I would spend at least an hour on the phone with Alice at her apartment in Houston. We talked about every facet of our lives, shared our life dreams with each other and prayed for God's will.

Alice's friends had told me of her deep commitment to the Lord. Her parents, Mr. and Mrs. Gene Day of Lake Jackson, Texas, sixty miles south of Houston, were longtime members of the First Baptist Church. Martha, Alice's mother, had taught Sunday School and faithfully served the Lord for decades. Before going to be with the Lord, Mr. Day was a beloved football coach. A football stadium in Lake Jackson was posthumously named after him.

Alice had been saved and had surrendered to the ministry at age 15. From the time she was saved, she began praying for her husband-to-be. I had begun to think I didn't have a prayer with her. Yet before we had ever met, she had been praying for me! Jim Bob Griffin, her former youth pastor, said she had a beautiful testimony. She was a treasure!

She was learning how to be an intercessor when I met her, although what that meant was not clear to me then. What *was* clear to me was her pattern of cutting short our dates for yet another prayer meeting.

Many dinners together, dozens of roses, reams of correspondence and several lengthy long-distance phone bills later, we were married. We didn't have a beautiful church wedding, which we still regret. Because of my schedule, we were married "on the run" between revival meetings.

HONEYMOON FROM HELL

The truth is we spent what was to be our honeymoon at a regional evangelistic crusade in Gulfport, Mississippi. It was going to be great—under the circumstances. We would be making a beautiful, leisurely drive up the Texas-Louisiana gulf coast to Gulfport, Mississippi, and stay in a nice hotel at the expense of the crusade. The usual hotel amenities would include daily maid service, a sparkling swimming pool and a gourmet restaurant where the food would be charged to our room. It was to be almost like a traditional honeymoon; we would just have to work each night.

At least that's the way I described it to Alice. But I was wrong. Very wrong!

A month earlier, a massive hurricane had demolished the coastal area, and the beaches along our "romantic" honeymoon drive were filthy, stained with tar and strewn with litter. The beautiful antebellum homes that once overlooked the sea walls had been reduced to rubble. Expensive yachts and sailboats lay splintered and sunk by the powerful storm. Others had been tossed like discarded toys in open fields.

Our "beautiful, leisurely drive to Gulfport" became an intercessory assignment! (Intercessors do things like this, you know.)

The biggest shock was yet to come. In an effort to save money, the churches sponsoring the crusade had secured a room for us at the local junior college, which was between semesters. The stark surroundings of the girl's dorm were not exactly what I had promised my beautiful bride.

Our room had twin beds and the Spartan atmosphere of a summer camp—complete with bugs! With me walking the halls, the few girls residing there for the summer were as nervous as long-tailed cats in a room full of rocking chairs.

Then there was the water. The tap water was brown! No kidding! The residents said it was normal for Gulfport, but it didn't look normal to me. When I took a tub bath, I felt like a marshmallow in a cup of hot chocolate!

It was disastrous.

A MAN'S WORLD

Evangelism is a way of life. And for the first couple of years of our life together, Alice merged her life, talents, and gifts with the itinerant ministry God had given me. We traveled 50 weeks a year conducting morning and evening services in churches and stadiums.

> The world of professional evangelism,
> dominated by male pastors and
> evangelists, was hard for Alice. But she
> accepted her role with grace.

The world of professional evangelism, dominated by male pastors and evangelists, was hard for Alice. Often discounted because she was a woman, she found herself in a new occupation, a new marriage and in a man's world. Though overwhelming to her at times, she accepted her role with grace.

Alice admits it was during this time that she really developed an intimate relationship with the Lord. In her isolation, she seized the opportunity to grow closer to God.

So, more than 300 nights a year and most mornings we were in revival or crusade services. On airplanes, layovers at airports, driving long hours by car or driving our motor home, our experiences while living on the road presented us many challenges in prayer. But that's another book!

CALVARY BAPTIST CHURCH IN HOUSTON

In 1982, Alice and I assisted in planting Calvary Baptist Church (now called Calvary Community Church) in northwest Houston. The church grew quickly, and the city came to know Calvary as a praying church. The Lord used Alice to mentor many at Calvary in the area of intercession.

Every Tuesday morning our senior pastor, Steve Meeks, would gather the pastors for several hours of worship and intercession.

God used these richly rewarding prayer times both to develop our team relationships and to reveal His direction for the church. He was also using these prayer times to train me in intercessory prayer.

Pastor Meeks and Calvary allowed Alice and me to construct a separate prayer ministry while serving on staff. At the same time, Alice and I were seeing the Lord enlarge our own prayer shield—those intercessors who were committed to pray for us and our ministry. Many of them continue to pray for us today.

THE U.S. PRAYER TRACK

In 1993, Peter Wagner called and asked me to consider coordinating prayer in the United States for the AD2000 & Beyond Movement.

"What would that involve?" I asked.

He explained that it would involve identifying and networking together existing prayer ministries in the United States for the purpose of world evangelization.

"How do you do that?" I asked.

"I don't know," he answered. "No one has ever done it before."

"What does it pay?" I inquired.

"Whatever you can trust God for," he answered calmly.

I told him I wasn't interested. "Pete, I need a real job." Hey folks, Alice and I had lived many years in evangelism never knowing where our next paycheck would come from. We had grown quite comfortable with our steady church salary.

"Would you at least pray about it?" Peter asked.

"Pete, I don't pray about things that don't interest me," I quipped.

To my complete surprise a month later, as Alice was into her 30th day of fasting for God's direction for our lives, Peter called again.

He said, "I can't get you off my mind. I believe you are supposed to do this."

I agreed to at least pray about it. Sure enough, as soon as I mentioned it to Alice, she enthusiastically said, "You're supposed to do that!"

"How do you know?" I inquired.

"Because of all the prophetic words, dreams, and visions our intercessors have given us over the past several years." She went to the closet and retrieved a three-ring binder. Page after page, some going back several years, described how God would be leading us into a new ministry, a national ministry, a ministry to ministers and other ministries.

One intercessor had written, "I was praying and felt God say that He has something for you to do that has never been done before." Then I remembered Pete's words a month earlier: "No one has ever done it before." This word was a profound confirmation.

Alice has since joined me as International Prayer Coordinator of the U.S. Prayer Track. I am amazed when I walk into our bustling offices and see our dedicated full-time and part-time staff members and the scores of volunteers.

Respected around the world as a leader in the intercessory prayer movement, Alice also serves on the International Reconciliation Coalition and the International Spiritual Warfare Network. Her book, *Beyond the Veil: Entering into Intimacy with God Through Prayer*, was published by Regal Books and has been well received. Almost daily we receive letters from men and women whose lives have been changed by the message of Alice's book.

WHY ME, LORD?

In Texas we have a saying: "When you see a turtle on a fence post, you can rest assured someone put it there." That best describes my feelings today. I have asked God repeatedly why Alice and I are involved at this level of prayer mobilization. I guess He grew so weary of the question that He startled me one day with His answer.

"If you must know why," He said, "then I'll find someone else." From that moment, I've left the reasons up to Him.

So I'm married to an intercessor. Alice and I have a strange and wonderful relationship. I'm strange and she's wonderful. Okay, so it's an old joke. Actually intercessors are strange! And wonderful.

Being married to an intercessor has presented our home and family with wonderful blessings—and its share of challenges. To meet these challenges, the Lord has helped me to learn what intercession is, who intercessors are and the Kingdom role God intends for them to play. Join me for a closer look at these amazing people.

2

An Intercessor? What's That?

Intercessors can travel further and faster in their prayer closet than on any form of modern transportation, serving as prayer missionaries to any nation on earth at any moment of the day. Dan Crawford, professor of prayer at Southwestern Baptist Theological Seminary, in his book *Connecting with God*, tells an exciting story of how powerful intercession can be.

One illustration of praying in the Spirit happened one Sunday in April 1912. On that night the Titanic struck an iceberg. Colonel Gracy, a passenger on the ship, after helping launch the few lifeboats that were available, had resigned himself to death. However, as he slipped beneath the waves, his wife at home was suddenly awakened with great concern for her husband. She prayed for several hours, until peace came. Meanwhile, Gracy bobbed to the surface near a capsized boat and eventually was rescued. He and his wife later discovered that during the very hours she was agonizing in prayer, he was clinging desperately to this overturned boat.[1]

Colonel Gracy was certainly blessed to have an intercessor for a wife!

WHAT IS AN INTERCESSOR?

People often ask me to define *intercessor*. "Who are they?" "What are they like?" "Any identifying marks or behavioral traits?"

Here's how to spot an intercessor. They are:

- Those who pray longer than anyone else.
- Those who pray the most often.
- Those who see prayer as a higher priority.
- Those who are usually the first to agree to pray for you.
- Those who rarely miss a prayer meeting.
- Those who derive the greatest fulfillment from praying.
- Those who are particularly sensitive to the traumas and moral decay in society and consider prayer to be a primary answer.
- Those who are anointed when they pray aloud.
- Those who carry God's burden and who experience travail.
- Those who are committed to developing prayer strategies, organizing prayer chains, etc.

WARNING: Intercessors tend to be a bit more radical and emotional than the rest of us. After all, many of them are on the cutting edge of what the Lord is saying and doing in the earth today!

ALICE GETS THE CALL

When Alice was saved at age 15, one of the first things God revealed to her was that she was to be an intercessor. But it wasn't until she received a copy of Rees Howells's *Intercessor* in the early 1970s that she learned what an intercessor and intercession really were.

Few models or mentors were available to Alice to lead her into the ministry of intercessory prayer. She learned largely by trial and error and by reading the few books available on the subject. Most of these books were the biographies of men—not women—and most were not contemporary.

Alice longed for a current example or teacher. When a burden from God would come upon her during a corporate prayer time, and her emotions and spiritual passion were stirred, the group would watch and evaluate her.

Like many budding intercessors today, Alice was often misunderstood. I couldn't help her because intercession was unfamiliar to me as well. Misinformation and lack of intercessory instruction are just two of the reasons many gifted intercessors have yet to identify and embrace their call to intercession.

The terms "intercessor" and "intercessory prayer" may be new to you. Most Christians are acquainted with devotional prayer which involves adoration, confession, thanksgiving and supplication. You are probably also familiar with the model prayer, or the Lord's Prayer, that Christ gave to His disciples (see Matt. 6:9-13).

WHAT IS INTERCESSION?

Intercessory prayer is "prayer ministry" on behalf of another person or persons. It extends beyond devotional prayer to the point where the pray-er comes before God to plead the case of another person or cause. The word "intercession" is from the Greek word *entugchano*, which means to confer with or to entreat in favor or against something or someone. Sounds like an attorney, doesn't it?

Jim Goll puts it this way:

We have God's permission and invitation to plead our case and make appeals in the courts of heaven before our great Judge and God. The dictionary definition of plead is (1) "to argue a case or cause in a court of law"; (2) "to make an allegation in an action or other legal proceeding," and a definition for plea is "an earnest entreaty."

The Hebrew word translated as "plead" in Isaiah's declaration is *shaphat.* It means "to judge, to pronounce sentence, to vindicate, to punish, or to litigate." The Hebrew word translated as "declare" or "state your cause" is *caphar,* which means "to score with a mark as a tally or record, to inscribe and also to enumerate: to recount, to number."[2]

Another Greek word similar in meaning to *entugchano* is the word *parakletos.* A *parakletos* is an intercessor, a consoler or advocate, a comforter. This word is used to describe the Holy Spirit, the Comforter that Christ promised to send us. As His attorney, the Holy Spirit or *parakletos* pleads the case of Jesus Christ to lost humanity. "He will testify about me," Jesus explained. "He will guide you into all truth" (John 15:26; 16:13).

The word *parakletos* also appears in 1 John 2:1 describing Jesus as our advocate with the Father. He pleads our case when we sin, as a lawyer would plead the case of an accused person before a judge and jury. Likewise the intercessory pray-er, or intercessor, pleads the cases of others in prayer before the very throne of God!

A Foundational Ministry

Every other ministry of the Church involves going to people on behalf of God. Intercession is the only ministry that involves going to God on behalf of people. Without it, other ministries will be little more than "cut flowers" that look good and smell good for a time. If not bathed with intercessory prayer, these ministries will wilt, having no roots. Intercession puts the power of God into the work of God!

Intercession is heavenly! It must, however, be balanced with the other more down-to-earth ministries. Having been the pastor of a church with a high proportion of intercessors, I affectionately had to remind my people that Jesus did a few other things between His prayer times. He healed the sick, cast out demons, raised the dead, and fed the hungry—just to name a few!

Just as some pastors love their studies, intercessors love their closets. To me, my closet is a place to hang my clothes. To Alice, it is a hallowed place of prayer. She finds her greatest fulfillment there. It's all a matter of perspective, isn't it?

Whether it is a pastor in his or her study, or an intercessor in his or her closet, to be cloistered away from real life can become escapism if we're not careful. We shouldn't run from life for the answer! We must run to life—*with* the answer!

A Priestly Ministry

Other religions have many members and few priests. Christianity is a religion of priests! Without exception, we are all priests unto God. The two significant duties of our priesthood today are worship and intercession, which happen to be the two principal activities of heaven (see Rev. 5:8-10).

When we pray the Lord's model prayer—see Matthew 6:9-13—we say, "Thy kingdom come, thy will be done on earth as it is being done in heaven." If we want that which is done in heaven to be done here on the earth, then it's up to us in part, isn't it? After all, Scripture says God is looking for two kinds of people: intercessors and worshipers (see Ezek. 22:30; John 4:23). We have been given the opportunity to become the answers to our own prayer!

Intercession is a priestly duty. In the Old Testament the priest would intercede before the Lord for the people (see Ezra 9:5—10:1).

This is also the case in other religions as well. Whether we speak of a Buddhist monk, an African witch doctor or an Indian shaman, these priests bridge the gap between the seen and the unseen worlds on behalf of their followers. However, the monks, the witch doctors and the shamans don't know the true and living God through His Son, Jesus Christ. Therefore, they stand providing a bridge between only the evil spirit world and their followers.

Christ, of course, is our High Priest (see Heb. 4:14). He is the Great Intercessor who pleads our case before the Father in heaven at this very time! (See Heb. 7:25.)

In the Old Testament we read of the Lord sending a plague upon the children of Israel as punishment for their rebellion. The Lord was extremely angry and told Moses to get out of His way; He was going to destroy them all. Desperately, Moses and Aaron fell on their faces before the Lord. Then Moses told Aaron, "Get up, fill your censer with fire from the altar and incense and carry it into the street among the people. Because of His anger, the Lord is killing them." So Aaron took incense and ran out into the streets. He offered the incense for the people's sin, stood between the living and the dead, and the plague was averted! (See Num. 16:44-48.)

In the New Testament we see Zechariah the priest, who was John the Baptist's father, offering incense at the time of prayer in the temple (see Luke 1:10). Incense represents prayer or intercession. Interceding, then, is a priestly assignment.

You may recall that the Levites, those of the tribe of Levi, were the priestly tribe of Israel in the Old Testament. But it may surprise you to know that God never intended for the tribe of Levi to be Israel's only priests. In fact, He invited the entire nation to enter the priesthood! He told the nation of Israel:

Now if you obey me fully and keep my covenant, then out of all nations you will be my treasured possession.

Although the whole earth is mine, you will be for me a kingdom of priests and a holy nation (Exod. 19:5,6).

His invitation for all of the Israelites to be His priests was contingent upon their obedience. You'll recall that sadly they never met His condition. They always proved to be disobedient. Only Levi and his family were finally employed as priests (see Num. 3:6-9).

Then in the New Testament, God makes an amazing announcement. He doesn't just *invite* believers to be priests. He *declares* us His priests! "But you are a chosen people, a royal priesthood, a holy nation, a people belonging to God, that you may declare the praises of him who called you out of darkness into his wonderful light" (1 Pet. 2:9). There are no conditions other than our salvation! Why? Because Jesus has met all the conditions on our behalf! (See Matt. 5:17.)

We are a kingdom of priests. Each of us is both capable and responsible to stand in the gap between the seen and the unseen, between the needs of men and God's supply until God meets their needs (see Ezek. 22:30,31). We are all to intercede. It's an awesome privilege.

A Diverse Ministry

Lest you think all intercessors are alike, nothing could be further from the truth. Like ice cream, intercessors come in many "flavors."

God's anointing will differ from intercessor to intercessor, as will their methods of praying. Some pray through lists, while others, like Alice, find lists to be restrictive. These people pray prophetically, that is they pray according to the prompting of the Holy Spirit. Once in their prayer closets, they just put the car in gear, then let the Holy Spirit drive.

Intercessors are also given differing assignments and goals. Some pray for cities or nations; some for social issues. Some pray for pastors and church leaders. Others pray for people in crisis and crisis situations. Alice tends to pray for church leaders (as God assigns them to her) and for the evangelization of the nations.

Intercession is not gender-biased. God calls both men and women to be His intercessors. It is true that the majority of those identified as intercessors today are predominantly female. However, history records that men are quite effective and necessary to this important spiritual ministry. Men will often employ more masculine qualities in their ministry of intercession. These qualities include a father's heart, linear thinking and logical strategies.

The intercessor's gender, spiritual gifts, talents, natural interests and assignments from the Lord will shape his or her intercessory style.

A Hidden Ministry

Although every Christian is to intercede for others in prayer, some are called to the ministry of intercession. The ministry of intercession is difficult for many to understand partly because it is a ministry that is largely performed in secret. (See Matt. 6:6.)

Content to remain nameless, faceless servants of the Most High, intercessors know they can reach higher from their knees than from a standing position.

These closeted intercessors are often uncomfortable with public ministry. They shun the limelight and have no interest in acclaim. They understand that, in His time, the Father who hears them in secret will reward them openly. Mostly content to remain nameless, faceless servants of the Most High, these praying people know that they can reach higher from their knees than from a standing position!

This was the case one Sunday morning in 1988. I was leading the worship at our early morning service when the Holy Spirit came in great power. His presence settled so powerfully on Calvary Baptist that morning that the people could barely stand. In fact, many lay facedown at the altar for hours, weeping and repenting before the Lord.

The early service continued on into the Sunday School hour. The ushers told those arriving for Sunday School, "God is here in an extraordinary way. There will be no Bible Study classes today. Go on into the auditorium."

An hour and a half later, it was time for the late worship service. Again, the ushers told those arriving, "Something unusual is happening. The Holy Spirit is here. Go on into the auditorium quietly and obey God."

During the morning many people went to the phones and called relatives and friends who had stayed home that day. "Get up. Get dressed. Get down here. God is here today!"

One husband and father was at home relaxing when his wife called from the church. "Get dressed and come down here, honey. The Lord is here and it is awesome!"

This fine man dressed and began driving toward the church. He stopped for a red light at an intersection. While he was sitting there, he looked across the street and saw a row of a dozen or so sapling trees that the landscapers had recently planted. There was a stiff wind blowing and every tree but one was bent almost double. That one tree was standing erect as though there were no wind at all. As he studied that tree he felt the Lord say, "The one tree you see that is unmoved by the wind represents YOU!"

He hurried to the church and rushed into the auditorium. Pressing his way through the overcrowded room, he fell facedown at the altar in repentance. God met him in a powerful way.

This dear brother shared with us the testimony of the trees. To this day, the marks of that encounter with God are still evident in his life!

Little did I know that, during this visitation of the Lord, Alice had seen an unfamiliar woman standing against the back wall praying. When Alice introduced herself and asked if she could help her, the woman told her this story:

> This morning when I awoke the Lord told me, "Go to Calvary Baptist Church because I am going to show up there in power. You are to stand at the back of the auditorium and intercede until I release you." I have never been to this church before. My family goes to the Methodist church down the street, but I knew God told me to come here. And look, He is here!

Seven hours later, after 18 adults received Christ as their personal Savior, and hundreds of Christians were touched by the presence of God, this hidden intercessor disappeared. To this day we do not know who she was, or where she lived. One crystal-clear fact remains. God speaks to His intercessors and they will risk all to obey. She wanted no thanks, needed no recognition and desired no credit. She was practicing simple obedience.

A Powerful Ministry

God has chosen to respond to His praying people. He moves in answer to their prayer. As my friend Alvin Vander Griend says, "God doesn't answer prayer . . . He answers praying people!"

Intercessory prayer is foundational and necessary for both life and ministry. Dr. Bill Bright, founder of Campus Crusade for Christ International, says he looks forward to the day when he is promoted from the presidency of this great ministry to the office of intercessor. What an awesome statement from a man of such prominence in the ministry!

During the last hundred years, we've seen the Church become everything *but* a house of prayer. Today, however, God is setting the stage for a divine intervention. In the past few years, He has initiated the greatest prayer movement the world has ever known. One prayer mobilizer said, "I find myself running around saying, 'Wait a minute, God. I'm suppose to be coordinating that!'"

Pastor Bob Beckett of Hemet, California, discovered a small group of intercessors that had given up public ministry fifty years before in order to pray for revival. For fifty years they had been nestled away from the world at the Throne of God, praying six nights a week in a mountain cabin. He asked one of the elderly ladies how she could abandon every modern convenience, give up personal pleasure and success and hide away in a mountain cabin to pray all these years. The elderly lady, one of the few surviving members of the original group, smiled at Pastor Bob. She looked deeply into his eyes and sweetly answered, "Surely young man, you haven't been with Him." Bob says he was reduced to nothing by her gentle, yet profound correction.

As a prayer leader, I am continually in the company of intercessors. I find most of them to be deeply committed Christians. They tend to experience a more passionate, intimate relationship with the Lord than most of us. This intimacy is obviously heightened by the hours they spend in His presence.

A Selfless Ministry

A unique quality shared by intercessors is an unselfish willingness to bear the burdens of others. True intercessors often spend less time praying for their own needs than they spend praying for the needs of others. They live a life of almost continual "spiritual pregnancy"; that is they are pregnant with a burden to see the Great Commission fulfilled.

Not unlike a husband who brings his work home from the office, intercessors can easily transfer their burdens, heartaches and spiritual discontentment to situations at home, to their families, spouses, churches, and yes, even to their pastors. However, I find that intercessors' wisdom to recognize this tendency and their courage to confront it make them effective and delightful people!

Not only do intercessors bear their own burdens and the burdens of others, they are frequently called upon to bear the burden of the Lord. However, when God chooses intercessors and entrusts the burden of His broken heart to them, it can be quite overwhelming. Failing to know that the burden they feel is of God, some intercessors wrongly assume they are weak, sick or, worse yet, wicked. Of course, this plays right into the hands of the evil one. Dear intercessors, do not let the enemy condemn or confuse you!

Alice and I have discovered that some Christians have confused experiencing the burden of the Lord with clinical depression.[3] However, when an intercessor properly carries a God-given burden into their prayer closet it should have been lifted when they emerge. If you are an intercessor and are constantly laden with a heaviness that won't lift, then it is likely you have other issues with which to deal. There may be a sin in your life that needs to be confessed, or the enemy may have given you a burden that creates a sense of hopelessness and even panic on some occasions. You may even have a medical problem.

A Warfare Ministry

Intercessors are warriors—prayer warriors. They are essentially discontented with the status quo. I call them God's spiritual activists. They're not driven to march in the streets, carrying placards and yelling slogans. Instead they are drawn to their prayer closets to weep and travail over the plight of others and the broken heart of God.

These precious sheep are disturbed by the condition of a world in the grip of Satan. The hearts of intercessors are filled with anger toward Satan (see Rom. 12:9), love for God and compassion for the oppressed. With a holy dissatisfaction, the intercessor lives in a state of righteous tension between the way things are and the way that God intends them to be.

A Shared Ministry

No longer are pastors the only persons in the local church with Kingdom vision, a view of the "big picture." More and more, intercessors are becoming acutely aware of God's activity in their churches, their cities and around the world. Individually and corporately they are crying out for revival and spiritual awakening. Some pastors may find it challenging, even a bit intimidating to lead such passionate, envisioned people. How is it intercessors are so informed and envisioned?

Hearing and answering God's call on their lives, more intercessors are discovering their spiritual gifts and recognizing their assignments. They are linking across denominational lines in cities across America. Praying people are networking via conference calls, faxes, Internet web sites and e-mail forums. As technology advances, so will the global prayer movement. More books, magazines, and newsletters dedicated to prayer and fasting are being published today than ever before! Hundreds of large prayer ministries across America produce informational and inspirational newsletters aimed at mobilizing intercessors.

Global Harvest Ministries, Harvest Evangelism and Gospel Light are among the many ministries offering national and international conferences on prayer and spiritual warfare. Tens of thousands have attended these training conferences organized by C. Peter Wagner, Ed Silvoso and others. Each year the number of such conferences increases in response to the demand.

In addition, denominations, prayer ministries, local churches and local intercessory prayer leaders are offering seminars, retreats and conferences on intercessory prayer. Never before has such prayer training been available to the Church!

Since 1990, the Church has witnessed an explosion of inter-cessory prayer. As Peter Wagner said at the Global Consultation on World Evangelism in 1995 in Seoul, Korea, "The global prayer movement is out of control!" More people are praying than at any time in history!

ABC's "Good Morning, America" recently sent a camera crew to Houston to interview some of us who are involved in prayer mobilization. But what impressed the producer most was the number of lay people involved in prayer walking our city. They videotaped a team of lay people walking through a neighbor-hood, praying over each home.

During PrayUSA! '98, I was interviewed by *Restaurant Business* magazine in New York City. They were asking the ques-tion, "How will the fasting of millions of Christians affect America's restaurant industry?"

During that 40-day fasting and prayer period, a major public relations firm reported 55 national media hits (nationally pub-lished articles or broadcast news reports) for PrayUSA!, including a front-page article in *The New York Times*.

Even the secular media is recognizing God's prayer initiative!

RESTORATION OF FASTING AND UNITY

The second half of this decade has seen restoration of the disci-pline of fasting. In December 1994, Dr. Bill Bright called 600 national leaders together to fast and pray for three days in Orlando, Florida. In November 1996, the third annual fasting and prayer event was held in St. Louis, Missouri. Christians every-where are fasting! Some people fast a day or two a week. It's common to find those who are fasting 10, 21, 30, even 40 days at a time.

Why is this increase in fasting significant? In Alice's booklet on fasting and prayer, *Power Praying*, she writes, "When fasting is added to prayer, something spectacular begins to happen!"[4]

Prayer and fasting are the primary tools God is using to bring unity in the Body of Christ. Pastors and churches are crossing racial and denominational lines to pray together. In so doing, they are forging the new, strong, sincere relationships necessary to fulfill the Great Commission. The walls that once divided us are falling down as surely as the Berlin Wall fell and is no more.

Christians today are living in a new day of spiritual understanding, awakening to their gifts and callings in unprecedented numbers. For 25 years, controversial gifts have severely divided the American Church. Today, however, the Body of Christ is rising to new levels of maturity. Sincere, mature Christians have learned there is strength in our diversity as well as in our unity. We are not enemies; we are family. The family of God!

Notes

1. Dan Crawford, *Connecting with God* (Fort Worth: Scripta Publishing, Inc., 1994), p. 5.
2. Jim Goll, *The Lost Art of Intercession* (Shippensburg, Pennsylvania: Destiny Image, 1997), p. 45.
3. Alice Smith, *Beyond the Veil* (Ventura: Regal Books, 1997), pp. 52-54.
4. Alice Smith, *Power Praying* (Houston: SpiriTruth Publishing, 1997).

3

Living with an Intercessor

In the mid-1970s, Alice and I went to see the movie *Jaws*. You may remember that *Jaws* was a huge box-office hit. By the time we arrived at the theater there were almost no seats left, so we were ushered to the front row. Now the front row of a movie theater is not like box seats at the ballgame. Sure, you have plenty of legroom, but to see the movie, you have to look almost straight up. Besides, everything on the screen looks super-huge!

As the lights went down, I leaned across Alice and jokingly said to the stranger sitting to the other side of her, "If anything strange happens, she's with you. Okay?" He smiled politely, but he obviously had no idea what I was talking about.

Jaws is about a rampaging, man-eating, 24-foot-long great white shark. The movie's writing, directing, editing and music work together to create increasing tension, the level of excitement growing with each frame. As the story unfolded a few feet in front of us, Alice became more and more tense. Soon she was gripping my arm, cutting off my circulation while I winced through each suspenseful scene.

As the movie approached its climax, the driving music becoming more insistent, the giant fish unexpectedly lunged through the side of a sinking cabin cruiser, baring its teeth, intent on making Roy Scheider its next meal. As the great fish sprang out of the water, Alice cringed. Everyone in the theater was breathless with suspense. And me? I bit my lip as Alice's sharp fingernails dug deeply into my knee.

A split second later, as the music peaked and it became clear that the fish had definitely missed the hero, Alice leapt to her feet, threw up both hands, and yelled at the top of her lungs, "Oh, praise God!" The packed auditorium burst into hysterical laughter. Despite my earlier plea, the man sitting next to Alice disavowed any knowledge of this woman.

THE FOUR BASIC PERSONALITY TYPES

My wife is radical about the Lord. She is particularly radical about prayer. You might say that she's *into* prayer! She'd rather pray than do just about anything. I intercede, but Alice is an intercessor. Prayer is her occupation, her hobby and her passion.

Christians, like most people, can be divided into four basic personality types: radical, progressive, conservative and traditional. Let's take a closer look at these personalities.

Radicals

Radicals are people who tend to be open, emotional, impulsive and easily excitable. They are radical about most of the things in their lives and are generally open to new ideas, to challenges and to changes. They are usually the first to try something new. Radicals will tend to elevate their emotions above their intellect.

It would be fair to say that the apostle Peter was a radical. Fishing naked (see John 21:7), denying Christ three times (see John 18:17-27), wanting to build a tabernacle on the Mount of Transfiguration (see Matt. 17:4), and cutting off a man's ear with a sword (see Matt. 26:51) are indeed radical acts!

Progressives

Progressives, of whom I am a card-carrying member, are more staid and stable than radicals. You might say we progressives border on perfection. Not! With the right provocation and after careful study, progressives can be motivated to risk and venture into new experiences. We sometimes lean toward apathy, and we tend to slip into "analysis paralysis."

Nehemiah might be a good example of a progressive personality. When he was given the bad report about Jerusalem's walls, Nehemiah didn't react impulsively. Unlike Peter, who would have packed his bags and immediately skipped town in order to repair the walls, Nehemiah "sat down and wept. For some days [he] mourned and fasted and prayed before the God of heaven" (Neh. 1:4). A person with a progressive personality most often responds to crisis this way.

Conservatives

Conservatives tend to be mildly resistant to change, more guarded emotionally and more passive by nature than progressives. Many conservatives want to see change—as long as they can also protect the traditions. Timothy, who pastored the church in Ephesus, was probably a conservative.

Paul exhorts Timothy repeatedly in issues of zeal. In 2 Timothy 1:6, Paul reminds Timothy to "fan into flame the gift of God." Later he illustrates the need to endure hardship "like a good soldier of Christ Jesus," and challenges Timothy to compete "as an athlete" (2 Tim. 2:3,5). Paul knew Timothy might slip into a passive role, as conservatives tend to do.

Traditionalists

Such words as "dignified" and "appropriate" come to mind when one thinks of traditionalists. As defenders of the status quo, traditionalists are the most resistant to change. They tend to suppress their emotions and elevate their intellects. Perhaps their theme song should be "We Shall Not Be Moved."

In order to walk in the Spirit (see Rom. 8:4) a spiritual person must never elevate his intellect, his will or his emotions above his spirit. Since the Holy Spirit resides in a saved person's spirit, the Christian's spirit must always rule his or her mind, will and emotions!

Along with your personality type, your spiritual gifts, age, income, culture, education and other factors contribute to who you are. We should never forget that God has made each of us unique, complicated beings!

MY RADICAL WIFE

As the story of *Jaws* illustrates, my precious Alice is a radical—she is radical about everything! This woman would rather watch the Houston Rockets professional basketball team play than eat. She was a cheerleader in school when her father was the football coach. Alice is a Dallas Cowboys football fanatic as well. When a Cowboys game is being televised, everything at our house comes to a screeching halt.

Now, I like football. I tend to watch the game casually from my recliner. I drink coffee, read the paper and talk on the phone during the game. Not her! Alice watches the game on her feet—even in our living room! Pacing, lunging, warning and encouraging the players and coaches, my radical wife is not bothered at all that they can't hear a word she's saying.

Some years ago when our youngest son, Bryan, was in the high school marching band, we went to one of the home football games. At one point in the game there was a goal line stand with the home team driving for a score. The entire stadium was electrified! Everyone was on their feet shouting and jumping up and down. Alice, my radical football fan, was oblivious to everything but the next play. Suddenly, beneath the roar of the crowd, I heard a smaller scream, more like a cry of desperation. Next to Alice, who was yelling at the top of her lungs, our four-year-old daughter, Ashlee, had gotten her head stuck in the iron handrail. In short order, Ashlee was freed and unhurt.

Oh, yes, the touchdown was scored, and Alice was happy.

It has been my experience that most—though not all—intercessors fall into the radical and progressive personality categories. The nature of the true intercessor is to be "on call" 24 hours a day, ready to weep between the porch and the altar like the prophet Jeremiah. The purpose of intercession is to see God change people and circumstances. That is a radical role! Certainly God has intercessors that would be considered conservatives and traditionalists, but they are "stealth warriors," laboring almost exclusively behind the scenes.

INTIMACY COMES NATURALLY TO INTERCESSORS

As warriors, intercessors must understand that the level of their spiritual authority is directly related to the level of their intimacy with Christ (see Jas. 4:7,8).

Intimacy has never come easy for me. Not being naturally affectionate, it requires work on my part. My brothers and I didn't hug and kiss while growing up. We were "macho"; we wrestled.

Alice, on the other hand, has a great propensity for intimacy. Her family is outwardly affectionate and closely knit. You can't imagine the shock I experience at her family reunions to find everybody kissing each other on the mouth!

My bride can be emotional, too. Tears come quickly and easily to her. Early in our marriage we struggled, as most couples do, with our differences. We tended to judge ourselves and one another according to our gifts and personalities. Measuring myself by her level of passion and her radical personality, I felt unfinished in my faith because my tears didn't come as quickly or as often.

One night early in our marriage, our "pillow talk" got around to this subject. Alice asked, "Why aren't you more openly affectionate?"

Like many husbands before me, I said, "You knew I was like this when you married me. What makes you think I'm suddenly going to change?"

About that time the Holy Spirit seemed to say to me, "Oh, are you beyond change?" He reminded me of Romans 12:2, where we are challenged to be transformed. I immediately repented to Him—and to Alice.

Today, most of my associates would characterize me as a fairly affectionate person, thanks to the conviction, the leadership and empowering work of the Holy Spirit, coupled with my own choice to be changed. An increased ability to express affection has also invigorated my prayer life!

SPIRITUAL GIFTEDNESS

You are a unique creation of the Father. He has made you the way you are. Assuming you love Him, He wants you to be comfortable being who you are. This is all part of His plan. Yet we sometimes judge ourselves and one another according to our own spiritual gifts or calling, in spite of Paul's admonition that one gift was never to be seen as superior to another (see 1 Cor. 12:21-24).

When your spouse is a gifted intercessor, it's easy to feel like a Volkswagen parked next to a Corvette when it comes to matters of prayer. Even before Alice and I were married, it was obvious we didn't pray alike. Jokingly I've said, "When I pray with Alice, I feel like a lost man." To be honest, her prayer life intimidated me.

Today I understand that the gift and the office of intercessor Alice possesses, along with her gender, personality and spiritual gifts, make her prayer life different from mine. These things make her effective on the level of prayer and the specific prayer assignments to which God has called her. Over time, I have grown to admire, not envy her.

As we have matured in our relationship with the Lord and with one another, both of us have learned to receive the other as a gift from God. We appreciate and honor each other, acknowledging our similarities and accepting, even celebrating, our differences all as part of God's plan!

TO COMPETE OR COMPLETE?

God is changing me in some areas. In other areas He's not changing me at all. Rather, He is using Alice's life to complete mine. We, like you and your spouse, are one flesh, one person. Alice is the other half of me.

If I succeeded in causing her to become like me, or if she succeeded in molding me to be like her, we would still be only half of what God intends for us to be! "As iron sharpens iron," God is using us to change each other, while preserving the individual qualities that make us unique (Prov. 27:17). This is happening in your marriage as well.

Just remember, intercession is a spiritual ministry, and living with an intercessor sometimes offers peculiar opportunities for "completion."

LIFE WITH ZEKE

What do you suppose it would have been like to be Mrs. Ezekiel, the prophet's wife? Early one morning, Ezekiel comes into the kitchen where his wife is cooking breakfast. Sheepishly, he asks her to sit down.

"Honey, the Lord woke me up last night," he says. "When I began to pray, He told me something I am supposed to do."

"Ezekiel, dear, you know I've always supported you in whatever you feel the Lord tells you to do. What did He say to you?"

"Well, it may seem strange, but God told me to take a sharp sword and use it as a barber's razor to shave my head and beard," Ezekiel calmly explains.

"You're to do *what?!*"

"God told me to shave my head and beard with a sword. But that's not all I'm supposed to do. I am to then take my hair, weigh it on a scale and divide it into three equal parts." (See Ezek. 5:1-4.)

Throwing her hands up in disbelief, Mrs. Ezekiel kvetches, "Now this is going too far! Ezekiel, do you realize what our friends are going to think? How am I going to explain this to my parents? Besides, how do you know it was God talking to you anyway?!"

LIFE WITH ISA

Consider for a moment Isaiah. Now there was some raw obedience! Can you imagine Mrs. Isaiah in the supermarket, when she overhears the conversation of two women on the next aisle?

"Sarah, did you see old man Isaiah in the parking lot a few minutes ago? He's lost it! I can't believe what I saw, or should I say what I didn't see!" Lucy says with shortness of breath.

"For heaven's sake, Lucy, tell me what Isaiah has done now!" prods Sarah.

"Well, you know how he's always going around town pronouncing judgments from God if we don't repent."

Sarah says sarcastically, "All he does is pray, fast and prophesy! Frankly, girl, nothing he does would surprise me. So hurry, tell me!"

"Well, you won't believe what he is doing now," Lucy says. "Isaiah is walking around naked—and I mean naked—through the streets. No clothes, no shoes. Naked!" (See Isa. 20:1-6.)

Sarah gasps, "Lucy, you have got to be kidding! No! Naked? I suppose he will tell us that God told him to do this, too! Imagine what his poor wife must think."

One aisle over, Mrs. Isaiah falls into the kosher foods display in a dead faint.

LIFE WITH THE MODERN-DAY INTERCESSOR

At times Alice has asked herself if she might be crazy. I frequently receive calls from intercessors, or those married to them, asking the same question!

I know husbands and wives of intercessors who have learned to live with some really radical behavior. Through the years, Alice has often been misunderstood, even misunderstanding herself at times. There were times she asked herself if she might be crazy. I frequently receive calls from intercessors, or those married to them, asking the same question.

As her husband, my job is to build up and encourage my wife. This has not always been an easy task because she's a complicated person. Alice is a warrior—a feisty, spirited scrapper. She hates the enemy, and he hates and fears her. Believe me, she is dangerous, especially when she's on her knees! Make no mistake, she's a lady. But while she's sometimes fragile and tender, she can be one tough cookie!

The ministry of prayer, particularly warfare prayer, can be difficult and exhausting. So it requires perception and sensitivity on my part to know how best to relate to her, when to press in and when to withdraw and give her space.

Chapter 3

WOMEN ARE FROM WHERE?!

I recently saw a bumper sticker that read, "Men are from Earth. Women are from Earth. Deal with it!" Peter wrote, "Husbands, likewise, dwell with [your wives] with understanding" (1 Pet. 3:7, *NKJV*).

Let's face it. Men don't understand women. So how can we be expected to understand our wives? I consider myself a perpetual student in a course entitled "Alice 101." I'm working toward a master's degree in the art of loving her and developing the skill of meeting her needs. This requires an open line of communication between us. It also demands a genuine desire of my heart as well as my reciprocal submission to her (see Eph. 5:21).

John Hagee, the pastor of Cornerstone Church in San Antonio, Texas, writes humorously about this in his book *Day of Deception*:

> A major problem is this: The husband sees the need of the wife, but his macho mentality says, "I'll hang on until she caves in." The problem with that *modus operandi* is that the little lady has a lot of spunk herself. She can get as mean as a junkyard dog. And then she eats his lunch. Soon, they are on the way to see the lawyer.
>
> Rather than submitting to each other, they have demanded their rights. I have seen it flair up a hundred times in a marriage counseling session. I call it a "rights fight." No family can survive a "rights fight." If you start saying, "my rights" and "her rights," it's over. Call the attorney and get ready to divide everything you have. Let me ask you a question: Do you want to be right or be reconciled?
>
> Much has been written about wives who marry men with the intention of changing them, but it really works

both ways. Many men think the same way: "I will marry her, then I'll change her." Read my lips, Leroy, it won't happen. There is not a verse in the Scriptures that says, "Husbands, change your wives"; nor is there a verse that says, "treat your wife like your oldest child."[1]

My desire is not to be right, but to be reconciled. Part of that reconciliation has been to learn that both our house and our children are extensions of Alice. The children literally came from her body. The house is her "nest"; it is an expression of her personality. In a real sense, her identity is wrapped up in our house. For a husband to ignore the children or fail to take care of a problem with the house is tantamount to ignoring his wife. They are both extensions of her.

Sir, to leave a burned-out light bulb unchanged, the sink faucet dripping, or to hesitate to pick up your son from soccer practice may seem unimportant to you. But it communicates to your wife that you are really ignoring her. (NOTE: The publisher should double the price of this book for that tip!)

Sometimes Alice just needs a look of love from me. Pastor Hagee says, "There is only one way to handle a woman. Richard Burton sang about it in the Broadway version of *Camelot*. 'How to handle a woman? Simply love her, love her, love her.'"[2]

At other times, Alice needs an affirming smile, a hug, a kiss or an embrace. Occasionally she needs a gentle word or a listening ear. Maybe she needs prayer, a compliment or encouragement. She may need something practical, such as assistance with household duties and the kids—or flowers!

If you are married to an intercessor, perhaps the two of you need to reassess your relationship in these areas. It may be that you will need to sit together and discuss these issues. You may also be called upon by the Holy Spirit to repent to each other for past attitudes and behavior. You may have become more of a hindrance to each other than a help.

A SPIRITUAL COVERING

As Alice's husband, I am a spiritual covering for her. For me to shield and defend her from spiritual attack is as important as protecting her from physical attack. I wouldn't tolerate any man trying to take advantage of her. So why would I sit apathetically by and allow her spiritual enemies (Satan and his minions) to take advantage of her? For me to be my wife's spiritual covering, I must cultivate a prayer life of my own in order to circumvent the enemy from dishonoring and intimidating her.

Praying regularly for my family's needs—and especially for Alice's—is one of my primary responsibilities. As Jesus did for His Bride, I am to love my wife and lay down my life for her (see Eph. 5:25). As He lives to make intercession for His Bride, I am to intercede for my bride (see Heb. 7:25). No, I am not the intercessor she is. But, like all Christians, I am responsible to pray.

And to pray effectively for Alice, I must know what is on her heart. What are her burdens? Her needs? As she bears burdens for the Lord and for others, it is my privilege to help bear *her* burdens. Again, this calls for communication.

Recently a discouraged wife approached me complaining that her husband sits idly by while their teenage boy screams at her. To her husband, who was standing beside her, I explained, "Because I love Alice, I would no more allow one of our children to scream at her than I would let the man next door scream at her." As her husband, I am to shelter and protect my wife both spiritually and physically.

To provide a proper spiritual covering for his wife, a husband must choose to live righteously in Christ Jesus. The husband is the primary gatekeeper of the family. As the family gatekeeper, he should be careful what he opens his life—the gate—to. Pornography, lustful thinking, anger and profanity are only a few of the areas in which some men open the door, allowing the enemy access to their families.

Of course, wives can also open the door for the enemy. Daytime television is filled with spiritual poison. It is impossible to obey Philippians 4:8 and feed on a steady diet of Ricky, Jenny, Sally, Geraldo, Jerry and the daily "sex operas," a.k.a. the soaps. We are accountable to God and must be accountable to each other. For what we allow into our lives, we also allow into our families!

Neither a wife nor a husband should look for emotional support from the opposite sex outside of their marriage. In God's design, the husband and wife complete each other, yet many married people today are guilty of committing "emotional adultery." A husband has no business sharing with his secretary—or his golfing or fishing buddies, for that matter—personal and intimate details concerning his wife or his marriage. Likewise, a wife has no business sharing certain things at the beauty shop, with her best friend or with the women's group at the church. Marriage partners should honor each other and hold such intimate things in sacred trust.

If you are struggling with intimacy in your marriage, you should seek out a godly marriage counselor or counseling minister with whom to share your concerns.

RELEASING ALICE TO THE MINISTRY

As a boy, I was always trapping animals and birds. About the time I would walk into the house with my newly captured prey my mother would say, "If you really love it, you must let it go, so it can live." Because I love Alice and want to see her reach her fullest potential in Christ, I release her to God's call upon her life. This call is not something that she has sought or something that we have generated. God is undeniably, divinely orchestrating it all! We are simply His stewards.

I've met several people through the years who desired to be released into areas of ministry, but there was little evidence of God's orchestration. Some were sincerely wanting to serve God, but were not in step with His timing. Some were ambitious, seeking significance in having a ministry of their own. Others were simply emulating other ministers. They were puzzled when their spouses or pastors would not bless and release them. Even their spouses were sometimes hard-pressed to explain why their reluctance. Often it was because there was too little evidence yet that God was involved in the move. Even if God has a ministry for you, it will likely require patience as you wait on His timing.

RELEASING HER TO THE CLOSET

Not only do I release Alice to love and pursue God, but I release her to the prayer closet. Perhaps I should say that I have released our closet to her! Her prayer closet has been our clothes closet.

For years our closet contained much more than our clothing. In it were a globe, maps, books, pens, photos, notebooks, Kleenex and other assorted items. The floor of our closet has literally been a workstation! When our children were younger, they thought God lived in our closet. Every time they'd look for Mom, I'd explain, "Mom's in the closet with the Lord, don't bother her."

One day Alice came walking out of the closet with mascara running down her cheeks. Her eyes were red and puffy. She was clutching a fistful of notes in one hand and a wad of used tissues in the other.

"What in the world do you do in there for three and four hours at a time?" I asked.

"Do you really want to know?"

"Of course I do," I replied.

"Then sit down," she said.

She began telling me the details of her encounter "beyond the veil" in prayer. I interrupted, "Whoa! Wait a minute! Let me get a pen and a piece of paper. People need to know this." I took notes as she shared.

When she finished, I gave my notes to her. "You must write a book about this for all the Church to read." She did. I mentioned earlier that her book, *Beyond the Veil,* is a source of affirmation and confirmation for many who've had similar experiences in prayer.

NEWS FLASH!

We've recently moved. Our new home has three walk-in closets in the master bedroom. I have my own clothes closet now! The third closet is Alice's new prayer closet.

RELEASING HER TO THE CHURCH

Not only have I released her to God and to the closeted ministry of intercession, but I have also released Alice to the Church. She is in demand as a speaker and is actually a wonderful preacher with a pastor's heart. The Father has released her from faithfully standing in the shadow of my ministry in order to effectively carry out her own.

In the fall of 1989, Alice had a powerful encounter with the Lord that would forever alter our lives. As an award-winning realtor in Houston, she was making more than twice my church salary. Furthermore, I had a top-paying staff position. God told Alice that in 1990, three months from that day, she was to shut down her successful real estate business in order to spend time in prayer. It was a very difficult time for her; not only was she successful, but she really loved the real estate business. Real estate was also an avenue for her to lead people to Christ. Alice had once been able to convince a couple who were divorcing and selling their house to recommit themselves to their marriage.

The Lord made several other demands upon her, but Alice alone understood the implications of them all. This was serious business. Indeed, she pondered in her heart most of what God told her and shared it with no one.

As instructed by the Lord, Alice arranged to close her business.

The following summer, a brochure for a church growth conference in Seoul, Korea, found its way into our hands. Neither of us had any real interest in church growth as a subject. Yet I sensed we were to attend this conference. We had a problem, though. Alice wasn't working; funds were tight. The good news is that again God intervened and supernaturally provided the money for us to go to Korea.

It was during this conference at Dr. Cho's Yoido Full Gospel Church, the world's largest church with more than 850,000 members, that Alice met C. Peter Wagner. Dr. Wagner is a prolific author and Fuller Seminary professor who, along with his wife, Doris, makes his home in Colorado Springs, Colorado. He is a leading authority on church growth, missiology and spiritual warfare prayer. In his book *Prayer Shield*, Peter describes the miraculous way he and Alice met. Within a few months, she became what Peter and Doris Wagner call their "I-1 personal intercessor."

Although I have never known Alice to seek promotion, I have watched as the Lord has elevated her from local church ministry to international ministry. It is now common for my wife to travel to the nations of the world without me.

RELEASING HER TO THE WORLD

Releasing my wife to God was difficult. Releasing her to the closet was more difficult. Releasing her to the Church was still more difficult. Now, I am learning to release her to the world!

Our friend Francis Frangipane coined a phrase, "New level, new devil." What that means to us is that the higher God lifts you in ministry, the higher the stakes. The higher the stakes, the higher the cost. Satan sets his strongest forces against those in leadership. Living with an intercessor who is also an international leader is a challenging responsibility.

We are living in dangerous days. Husbands and wives need to be committed to each other, united in their pursuit of Christ and committed to stand united against the enemy. Having one heart and one mind—the mind of Christ—they should love, honor and defer to each other by lifting the other in daily prayer.

Notes

1. John Hagee, *Day of Deception* (Thomas Nelson Publishers: Nashville, 1997), p. 142.
2. Ibid.

4

God Wants YOU, Too!

*I*t was early morning and the fog was still hanging mysteriously near the forest floor that surrounded our northwest Houston home. I drove slowly to the church where I was to address a large group of Christian women on the subject of spiritual warfare.

As I sat idling at a stop sign, something above me caught my eye. High above the street, precariously balanced on an electrical wire, was a squirrel. Tilting forward and backward, swaying first to the left, then to the right, the squirrel carefully inched its way across the street using its furry tail as a tightrope walker would use a parasol.

This amazing squirrel was midway across the wire when out of the fog came a crazed mockingbird. Like a World War II fighter plane, the bird strafed the startled squirrel, pecking it on the head. A bit dazed, the assaulted animal gathered its composure, turned cautiously and headed for the other side of the street.

As you can see, it doesn't take much to entertain me. Early for my meeting, I turned off the engine, climbed out of my car and sat down on the hood to watch this breathtaking aerial act. It was better than the Ringling Brothers-Barnum & Bailey Circus!

Again and again, the mockingbird would circle, then dive out of the fog, striking the confused squirrel on the head with its sharp beak. After each attack, the squirrel would reel, find its balance, then desperately try to reach the opposite side. Finally, in a risky maneuver, the squirrel lunged for the closest electrical pole. Then it raced headfirst down the pole and into a bush. All the while, the mockingbird continued its relentless air attack.

When at last I headed down the road, the last thing I saw in my rearview mirror was that bird diving into the bush for one more strike against the squirrel.

YOU ARE DANGEROUS!

At the conference, I relayed the story of the mockingbird and the squirrel. I wrapped up the story by asking the audience this question: "When it comes to spiritual warfare, how many of you can relate to that squirrel?" Perhaps recalling the spiritual migraines they had received from the enemy, almost without exception they nodded, smiled and lifted their hands.

Leaning across the lectern with a smile, I said, "Not me. I relate to the mockingbird. God didn't put me here to get headaches from Satan; He put me here to *give* Satan headaches! I am dangerous!"

It's true. Where Satan is concerned, whether or not you're a gifted intercessor, you are dangerous in prayer! Too many Christians today have more belief in Satan's ability to steal, kill and destroy than they have faith in Christ to destroy the works of the devil. As the Father sent Christ, even so He sends us into this world to pull down satanic strongholds, to wreak havoc and to annihilate the kingdom of darkness (see Luke 10:19).

Satan fell as a result of the rebellion he led against God in heaven. As his punishment, God deported him to earth. You see, for anyone who has known the glories of heaven, anything less than heaven is severe punishment. When Jesus encountered demonic spirits during His earthly ministry they asked Him, "Are you here to punish us before our time?" (See Mark 1:23-26.) The answer was most assuredly "Yes!" (See 1 John 3:8.) It is true, there is coming a time of perfected punishment for them (see Rev. 20:10); however, their punishment has already begun! And we have the privilege to assist in carrying out the sentence against these wicked workers of iniquity.

God didn't put us here to live as "spiritual squirrels," sitting passively or, worse, balancing precariously on the tightrope of life while praying for protection. No! We're not mere survivors. God says we're even more than conquerors; we're overcomers! (See Rom. 8:37; 1 John 4:4.)

It is not your job to hold on with hope. You are here to fight on with faith! God put us here to be His mockingbirds. Through our faithful obedience to Jesus Christ, we can give Satan a holy headache! We are to be Satan's worst nightmare. And the gates of hell SHALL NOT prevail against us! (See Matt. 16:18.)

A SPIRITUAL AVIARY

What kind of "spiritual bird" have you been? I am afraid that too many in the Church today are just standing around like the proverbial ostrich; they have their heads in the sand, spiritually speaking. They're almost oblivious to what God or the devil is doing in the earth. Furthermore, their view of Satan seems to be "If I can't see him, he can't see me. If I don't bother him, he won't bother me."

Other Christians are flitting around from conference to conference, seminar to seminar like hummingbirds flitting from blossom to blossom. They are always looking for their next sip of spiritual nectar. They never plug into the Body of Christ and meaningfully relate to its members. They're much too spiritual for that!

Some Christians could be likened to the wise old owl. They are consumed with learning. But Solomon wrote in Ecclesiastes, "I have grown and increased in wisdom . . . I have experienced much of wisdom and knowledge. Then I applied myself to the understanding of wisdom, . . . but I learned that this, too, is a chasing after the wind" (Eccles. 1:16,17). Much of the Church is so busy studying what God did in the past that they're not even aware of what He is doing in the present!

As pastor and author Steve Meeks has said, "The Bible is not the meat, it's the menu! The meat is in the street. Too many Christians are eating the menu and not the meat." Steve means no disrespect to Scripture. He is reminding us that acquiring spiritual knowledge should not be seen as an end in itself. We are to be about the business of extending the kingdom of God!

Finally, there are those Christians who are living as spiritual buzzards. Like scavengers, they look for dead or dying things. Rather than offering joyful, loving encouragement, they continually offer criticism and condemnation. Rather than soar with the eagles, they circle with the vultures. They are a drain on the Church and a reproach to Christ.

No! Even if you are not called to be a gifted intercessor, you *are* called to be as that mockingbird was to the squirrel. You are to be dangerous through Christ in prayer!

An Army of Intercessors

You may not consider yourself a gifted intercessor. Though intercessory prayer is not every Christian's ministry, it is definitely every Christian's privilege and responsibility. Today God is recruiting an army of intercessors, and all of us have been drafted. Let's put on our uniforms and report for duty! As Steve Bell, the chairman of PrayUSA!, says, "Today, many of us who have been converted to Christ, are being converted to prayer."

Some believers are especially called of God to a ministry of intercession. C. Peter Wagner defines the gift of intercession in his book *Your Spiritual Gifts Can Help Your Church Grow.*

> The gift of intercession is the special ability that God gives to certain members of the body of Christ to pray for extended periods of time on a regular basis and see frequent and specific answers to their prayers, to a degree much greater than that which is expected of the average Christian.[1]

A person who has the gift of intercession will have a greater prayer anointing on his or her life. I believe this anointing of intercession is also given to groups of people, to churches, to cities, even to nations. Several years ago, during the first International Conference on Prayer and Spiritual Warfare in Anaheim, California, Alice and I served on the intercessory prayer team. Together we prayed from 3:00 until 6:00 A.M. I had never prayed so long before in my whole life! Yet we seemed to have no sooner started than we were finished. It was powerful! In the sports world, they would say we were "in the zone." We were actually caught up into the realm of the Spirit, engaged with God in prayer. Time and space had lost all significance. There was an anointing, a supernatural grace to pray with that group of devoted intercessors. Corporately we had an inner knowledge that great things had been accomplished.

Heaven-sent grace to pray is common among gifted intercessors. It might be referred to as a call to intercede, not unlike the call to preach. It is intercession moved to the front burner—high priority! To them prayer is a first response, not a last resort.

Sometimes an intercessor's spouse "unplugs" from prayer, trusting the intercessor to do all the praying for the family. True, the intercessory prayer warrior doesn't need prodding. But this overreliance on the family intercessor can produce lethargy in the prayer life of the spouse as he or she assumes their "praying spouse" will handle every spiritual crisis that arises.

Since intercessory prayer is not my primary ministry, my prayer life is very different from Alice's. Her relationship with God is based largely on the image of being the Bride of Christ. After all, she knows what it's like to be a bride. She knows how a bride feels and how a bride is to act.

On the other hand, I see my relationship with the Lord as that of a son of God. My dad, Dr. Robert E. Smith, is a godly father. He has spent more than 50 years in pastoral and denominational ministry. Thanks to him, the easiest way for me to relate to God is as my Father.

Conversely, those who have grown up with a poor "father-child" relationship may have difficulty approaching the heavenly Father in this way. Jesus opened another relational door for them when He said, "Henceforth I call you . . . friends" (John 15:15, *KJV*).

How we come to God is not nearly as important as that we *do* come to Him. When we draw near to Him, He draws near to us. (See Jas. 4:8.) In the process of entering God's presence we are changed into His likeness. It is "transformation by adoration"! You may not be an intercessor, but this should not prevent you from experiencing a full and meaningful prayer life.

Prayer is no more a spiritual option for a Christian than breathing is a physical option. Prayer is a function of Christ's life in us. When Christ, *the* Intercessor, comes into our lives and is allowed to be Himself in us, He prays!

However, each person's prayer life is personalized. You must, as some say, find your own rhythm of prayer. Your personality, spiritual gifts and uniquely personal relationship with the Father determine it.

My prayer life has changed, deepened and increased since I

was born again at age five and a half. Let me suggest a few ways I have experienced God in prayer that might assist you in cultivating a deeper relationship with the Lord.

KEEPING A PRAYER JOURNAL

Prayers can be written, spoken, or silent. King David's prayer and praise journal is known today as the book of Psalms.

David didn't have a problem expressing his heart as many men do. For even the most verbose men, the hardest words to find are often those words that express intimacy or confront authority. Prayer, of course, entails both expressing intimacy and confronting authority.

From birth, men are taught that they are to be strong. Prayer is an activity that flies in the face of that instruction. As evangelist Mickey Robinson says, "Prayer is weakness." Many men have found that writing—or journaling—their prayers has liberated their prayer life. This might help you, too.

PRAY WITHOUT CEASING

Prayer is like breathing—you can do it while you do other things. I try to maintain the constant awareness of God's presence throughout the day, communing with the Father from moment to moment, from issue to issue. I acknowledge Him when blessings come and cry out to Him when I am challenged. He and I walk and talk together. In 1 Thessalonians 5:17, Paul describes this as ceaseless prayer.

For me it's never been so much a question of what would Jesus do if He were here. It's more of the question, *Jesus, what are You going to do since You are here?* We are to assume His presence, not His absence!

When I am in this mode, the Holy Spirit continually prompts me to pray for people and situations. Our prayer response to such prompting and directing by the Holy Spirit is known as prophetic praying.

KEEPING A PRAYER LIST

Then there are my appointed prayer times when, after a time of worship and adoration, I pray through my personal prayer list, those prime prayer assignments God has given me. My list includes me, Alice, our family, my elders, my deacons, my friends and their situations. Important events, pastors and various Christian leaders for whom I am committed to pray also appear on my list.

Some people find that by using a 3x5-inch card file with dividers they can best organize and keep track of their personal prayer list. The Rolodex system that holds cards in place as you flip them over one at a time is even better.

My prayer list is a file in my computer, as well as a marquee on my computer's screen saver. After a few minutes of inactivity—the computer's, not mine—my prayer list begins to slowly and continuously scroll across the monitor. At various times during the day it will catch my eye, and the Lord will touch my heart to pray. Right then I stop and pray for those people and situations that have captured my attention.

What do you do with a prayer list that has become too long? First, read through the list to determine whether the Lord has still assigned this need to you. Remember, you must always resist becoming need-driven and remain Spirit-led. Never let people and needs establish your agenda. The Lord alone must do that.

When the list gets lengthy, divide it into two parts and pray every other day for each part. Longer lists may need to be divided even further. Some people have a different list for each day of the week. In that case, you must trust God with the issues that don't fall on the day you are praying. God can raise up prayer support as needed. Your job is not to determine the level of prayer support, but to pray as God leads you.

Because my job as a prayer coordinator is prayer-related, many people assume that I am an intercessor and ask me for prayer. If I took every assignment, my prayer list would be a mile long! Sometimes I simply explain that I cannot accept the assignment. It is difficult to say no to a request for prayer. However, honesty is always the best policy. It isn't right to agree to pray for someone when I'm fairly certain that I can't or won't.

My usual practice is to pray for a person at the time of their request. I will say, "Yes indeed. Let's pause right now and ask God to intervene on your behalf." Then I pray for them on the spot.

Another way is to agree to pray for a specific length of time. That may vary from three days to a week or more. The Lord may release me after that time or lead me to continue interceding. My prayer assignments usually have a "life span." When the Lord releases me from one, it is removed from my list. How do I know when the assignment is over? It's simple. There is no more life left in it. As Alice says, "When the horse dies, dismount!"

PRAYING THE SCRIPTURE

Praying the Scripture offers you an endless supply of prayer directions and topics. You can take almost any Scripture passage and read it, meditate on it, personalize it, form it into a prayer and pray it back to God. God has told us to pray according to His will and He will hear us. 1 John 5:14 says, "If we ask anything according to his will, he hears us." Nothing more closely expresses the will of God than the Word of God!

PRAYING THE NEWS

You can also try praying as prompted by the world around you. Television, newspapers and radio can provide excellent prayer prompts. Watch the television news? No, I pray the television news! When I see and hear of a crisis, I immediately intercede. When I read the news report of a breakthrough for righteousness, I stop and thank the Lord for it.

> Make prayer a daily,
> moment-to-moment
> adventure in your life.

There are other kinds of prayer prompts, or "triggers" as Alice calls them. For example, highway signs and billboards can prompt you to pray creatively. A yield sign might provoke a prayer like, "Lord, it is my desire to yield all that I am to you today." A stop sign might prompt you to pray, "Lord, I pray that you'll stop Satan dead in his tracks in this neighborhood today." A Miller Lite beer billboard might have you praying, "Lord, I pray that you'll quench the thirst of every person named Miller in this city with your Living Water."

Make prayer a daily, moment-to-moment adventure in your life.

WHERE AND WHEN TO PRAY

Prayer times that work well are when I am walking, exercising or driving—with my eyes open, of course. (Don't be like the guy in Texas who, while traveling down the freeway at 70 miles an hour on his way to a picnic, put his van on cruise control so he could go to the back of the van to check on his iced watermelons. Hello-o-o! Anyone home?)

Some folks think that unless they travail for hours in prayer, they haven't really prayed. Intercessor, don't make your spouse think he hasn't prayed because his prayer style and endurance are not like yours. Prayers that raised the dead and called down fire from heaven in Scripture took less than a minute to pray. Jesus prayed briefly at His baptism, the heavens were opened and God spoke audibly!

I will, however, sometimes set aside an entire day of prayer. That day, all other business is suspended, and the entire day is spent in our prayer room. Church friends, our personal intercessors and our staff join me as they are able. But this is, first and foremost, a personal commitment born out of many needs that beg for prayer, my need to spend time with the Lord and my need for personal discipline. It is always time well spent, even in the midst of a busy schedule.

You can pray any time in any place. But those who are most successful in prayer have:

- An effective place for prayer
- An effective time for prayer
- An effective plan for prayer
- A record of prayer requests and answers to prayer
- An expectant spirit
- A submissive heart.

PRAYING TOGETHER

Late one night, fire destroyed a luxury home in our neighborhood. Each day on our way to work we passed the gutted remains.

For months we watched as our neighbors, their insurance company and contractors surveyed the damage, settled the claim, cleared the land, signed contracts, ordered the materials, secured the permits, hired a crew and waited for good weather to rebuild the house that had burned down. It took nine months to rebuild what the fire had destroyed in 30 minutes.

One day as I watched the construction progress, the Lord said to me, "Time is running out. What can be strategically destroyed in one hour of praying, Satan has neither sins, sinners nor time left to rebuild!" Amen!

If you're the husband or wife of an intercessor, can you begin to appreciate the critically important work to which God has called your spouse? Yet there's no need for you to feel threatened. You are both on the same team. Together you can both effectively destroy the works of the devil in the name of Jesus.

One intercessor can put 1,000 to flight. But an intercessor with his or her spouse can put 10,000 to flight! (See Deut. 32:30.) Could it be that God has coupled you with an intercessor to increase the effectiveness of your own prayer life? I am convinced that's one of the reasons God gave Alice to me.

YOUR SPIRITUAL GIFTS

You may not have a primary ministry of intercession, but you do have spiritual gifts (see 1 Cor. 12). God can use you and your spiritual gifts in intercession as conduits through which prayer can flow. He uses me, and He will use you if you are willing. There are several ways your ministry gifts can be more effective when you couple them with prayer. Let me share with you from my own experience.

Intercession and Evangelism

For centuries, the Church has tried to do the work of evangelism without focused, fervent prayer. Argentine revivalist Edgardo Silvoso says, "Trying to evangelize the lost without effective, focused, fervent, corporate prayer is like trying to show a highway sign to a blind man!"

One cold, bone-chilling day outside of Riga, Latvia, a former Soviet nation, our ministry team from the U.S. had just finished sharing the gospel with a roomful of beautiful elementary students. The principal, speaking through our interpreter, invited us to the teachers' lounge for refreshments. Latvian people are wonderfully hospitable.

As happens from time to time during the winter in Riga, there was no heating oil. It was bitter cold inside the school building, and the teachers' lounge was a tile room with a concrete floor. Bundled from head to toe, our ministry team stood around the room shivering and watching our breath, until one of the teachers brought in a tray with steaming hot coffee and homemade cookies. We ate somewhat quickly, thinking only of getting out of the cold. Then thanking them politely, I announced our departure.

Before turning to leave, I asked permission to pray for the teachers. It was so cold, I prayed quickly and almost unconsciously, asking the Lord to bless the three women and thanking Him for the kindness they had shown to us. The interpreter didn't try to interpret the prayer.

When I finished, one of the teachers pointed to me and in Latvian said, "You're a very powerful man."

"Ask her what she means," I said to the interpreter.

She asked the teacher, then explained to me, "She said that while you were praying for her, something broke off of her head and floated away."

I said, "Tell her that God touched her and ask if she would like to feel God's touch again."

The interpreter asked. The teacher nodded.

I walked across the room to her. "May I place my hand on your shoulder while I pray for you?" I asked. With her permission, I prayed that God would reveal the gospel to her—and He did! She prayed to receive Christ, then instantly burst into a broad smile and began to dance joyfully around the tiny room.

At that point I asked the other young teacher, "Would you also like to become God's child?"

Her head dropped. She stared at the floor and mumbled

something. The interpreter asked again, then explained, "She said she is a shy woman."

"Tell her God loves His shy daughters. Ask her again if she would like to be one."

Our interpreter gently asked her for me. The teacher nodded. I led her also in the sinner's prayer. In a moment she, too, was dancing with the first teacher in circles around our team. The cold chill had dissipated and that teachers' lounge suddenly seemed strangely warm.

Prayer removes the veil that blinds the minds of unbelievers in order that the gospel can be revealed to them (see 2 Cor. 4:3,4).

Intercession and Exhortation

Counseling, or exhortation, is my primary motivational gift. But in 38 years of ministry, I have noticed that man's counsel has, at best, limited ability to truly help someone.

Years ago it was my practice to make weekly counseling appointments with people that in some cases continued for months. The initial interview typically began with the person completing a 17-page fact-finding form. After all, I had to discover the real problem. The trouble is, the victim is usually the last to identify the real problem! If the person had known the real problem, he would have solved it long before and there would be no need for a 17-page form.

In the past, I counseled for 55 minutes and prayed 5 minutes. Today, I tend to pray for the person for 55 minutes and counsel with them for 5 minutes. I find that God does much more in one hour of prayer than I can do in weeks of counseling.

What had I been talking about for 55 minutes in counseling? I was telling people, of course, what they should be doing and thinking. But if they were capable of doing and thinking those things, they wouldn't have needed me in the first place! Yet, fully impressed with myself, I would spend the last five minutes in prayer, asking God to bless what I had just told them!

Thankfully, some people were helped. Today it is a different story. Before even seeing the person, I spend time in intercession for them. "Lord, what do you want to do today? What are you saying? Please show me the real problem!"

After all, Jesus said, "But when he, the Spirit of truth, comes, he will guide you into all truth. He will not speak on his own; he will speak only what he hears, and he will tell you what is yet to come" (John 16:13).

One woman drove from Dallas to my office in Houston for counseling. Arriving on a Saturday because she couldn't afford to skip work, she was desperate! I showed up at my office 30 minutes early for the appointment. Dimming the lights, I sat down at my desk in meditation.

I said, "Lord, I don't know this lady. I've never seen her. I don't know anything about her. You know everything about her. Do You wish to reveal anything to me about her? Is there any assignment You have for me regarding her today? Your Word says, 'Jesus gave them this answer: "I tell you the truth, the Son can do nothing by himself; he can do only what he sees his Father doing, because whatever the Father does the Son also does'" (John 5:19).

Nothing exciting happened. In fact, nothing at all happened for 20 long minutes! Then I vaguely saw two dancing cowboy boots flitting across my closed eyelids. That was it! Now that's what I call seeing through a glass darkly! (See 1 Cor. 13:12.)

"Two cowboy boots? What could that possibly mean, Lord?" I complained. Then it seemed to me I heard Him say softly, "Ask her about the country western dance." The Lord never seems to give us enough revelation to build our self-confidence. We never know enough that we become independent. He loves being pursued and reveals only enough to keep us seeking hard after Him!

A few minutes later the lady in question walked in and sat down. Obviously familiar with the counseling routine, she asked, "Well, what do you want to know about me?"

"Nothing!" I answered. "First of all, I think it's only fair to tell you that I can't help you. I've never helped anyone. Unless God chooses to do something today, you just wasted a trip down here." That had to be disappointing news after a five-hour drive from Dallas.

"Please don't tell me anything about yourself," I continued. "It will only confuse me. I only want to know the answer to one question. What in the world happened at the country western dance?"

Immediately, she burst into a river of tears and screamed, "Who told you about that?" Shell-shocked, I waited as she pulled herself together. Then it all spilled out. "I was saved in a revival meeting in my church when I was 15 years old. Two weeks later I was invited by a girlfriend to attend a country western dance. I knew I shouldn't have gone. I hesitated, she insisted, and finally I agreed to go.

"That evening at the country western bar, I made my way to the women's restroom. As I walked into the crowded restroom, a stall door opened. To my complete amazement, out staggered my Sunday School teacher. She was drunk and held a bottle of beer in her hand. I left that Sunday School teacher—and God—at ✳ that dance. I told God, 'If this is all there is to Christianity, You can have it.' Since then, my life has been a living hell. I am hopelessly addicted to alcohol and illegal drugs. I've had multiple marriages, and I'm totally miserable."

I asked if I could pray with her. As I did, God mended the broken pieces of her life. Husband or wife of an intercessor, if God can use *me* like this, I know He will use you!

Perhaps you are unable to develop a meaningful prayer life because of past wounds. Stop right now and let the Holy Spirit heal you. Repent of unconfessed sin. Release any offenses committed against you by others and ask the Lord to cleanse you today. (See Matt. 6:14,15.) Now open your heart to the new love relationship the Lord has for you through prayer.

GOD WANTS TO USE YOUR SPIRITUAL GIFTS

Whether or not you are an intercessor, God wants to use your spiritual gifts and your personality in effective prayer.

When I was a boy I lived to tear up stuff! My parents could never have a decent lawn because of my incessant digging in the back yard. Weird I know, but I was convinced that I could dig to China were I given a decent shovel! We lived in a part of Texas where there are no trees. My brothers and I had no choice. While kids in other cities had treehouses, our clubhouse was underground!

Even today I wake up in the morning with the hope that I can tear down something Satan has built. I was born for this job!

Note
1. C. Peter Wagner, *Your Spiritual Gifts Can Help Your Church Grow* (Ventura: Regal Books, 1979), p. 68.

5

Home Improvement

*I*ntercession is a spiritual enterprise, not without its share of problems. When Alice and I were first married, we seemed to be a real mismatch when it came to prayer. I'd typically pray first. This seemed to be the "husbandly" thing to do. It didn't take me long to pray my prayer.

Then Alice would pray.

I remember one night when the intercessory anointing came upon her so strongly that she was almost instantly in tears. Intensity began to build and she dropped to her knees beside her chair. I knew we were in real trouble then! Before long she was facedown on the carpet, caught up into the Throne room, crying out for mercy for something or someone on the other side of the globe.

After assessing the situation, I quietly tiptoed out of the room, walked downstairs and finished watching the news. You see, I was about as useless to what she was doing as a bowling ball without finger holes!

Seriously, I have learned to be at ease both with who Alice is and who I am. God made us both and designated us for His own purposes. Yes, she usually takes those "heavy-duty" assignments into her prayer closet. That is, unless God has given it to both of us.

INTIMIDATION

You, too, may have felt intimidated at times by your spouse's prayer life. It's hard to imagine the frustration of a person whose praying spouse intentionally *tries* to intimidate them. I've known intercessors to treat their husbands or wives like spiritual dwarfs or ignoramuses. Manipulating your spouse with self-pity, by holding personal secrets ("I can't tell you, because you just wouldn't understand") or seeking to exalt yourself only creates jealousy and anger in the one you love.

Often the cycle of marital tension between an intercessor and spouse can begin when, with great excitement, the intercessor shares with his wife some deep spiritual insight he gleaned during a prayer time. The wife, unable to grasp her husband's revelation, may respond by feeling inferior and threatened. The intercessor may then sense rejection from his wife, even if her feelings are unspoken. The truth is, she is likely not rejecting her intercessor husband, but rather the unfamiliar spiritual realm that the intercessor accepts as quite normal.

If the intercessor were to present such revelation logically and clearly to his spouse, this could prevent misunderstandings and alleviate a great deal of frustration for both partners.

NEGLECT OF THE HOME

Arriving home from work one day, Ben sensed something wasn't quite right the minute he walked in the door. The house was a mess. Clothing was strewn across the bathroom floor, shoes were blocking the doorway and the kitchen sink was filled with dirty dishes. The beds were unmade, and piles of laundry were stacked in the hallway like the pyramids of Egypt!

When he walked into the master bedroom, there was Sandra, his wife, still in her pajamas with no makeup and a headful of curlers. She was sitting in the middle of the bed, surrounded by Bible commentaries, Bibles, cassette tapes, notebooks and pens.

Exasperated, Ben blurted out, "Sandra, for goodness' sake, have you seen this house?!"

Smugly, she answered, "Ben, when will you fall in love with Jesus like me?"

Just as some pastors have neglected their families by using their ministry as an excuse, so too can an intercessor. Whether one is a pastor or an intercessor, his or her primary ministry is in the home. If the pastor or intercessor fails to be the person he or she should be at home, little else really matters.

PUSHING PRAYER

Frustration can also arise when the intercessor pushes prayer on the family, expecting other family members to share his or her burden. It's terrible when a parent uses prayer as a punishment ("Go to your room and spend some time in prayer!").

Likewise, it can be a disaster when a parent turns the family prayer time into a "prayer-a-thon." A good rule for the family altar is for everyone to pray at or near the level of the weakest or the youngest member. It is certainly not the time to "catch up" on your personal prayer time or your intercessory assignments.

If you are feeling manipulated by your spouse, it is important that you tell her. Communicate! Explain clearly what she is doing and how it makes you feel. It may be unintentional. Just making her aware of the problem may put the whole issue to rest.

On the other hand, you may need to develop an account-ability system that allows you to bring these behaviors to your spouse's attention when they appear. One couple worked out their own system. When the intercessory spouse begins "pushing prayer," the other holds up an index finger and smiles. This way they are able to communicate without conflict. Alice and I have found that prayer for each other and good communication solves lots of problems.

WHAT IF YOUR SPOUSE IS LOST?

I have counseled men and women who were not Christians, but were married to intercessors. The Bible calls this being "unequally yoked" (see 2 Cor. 6:14). It is often a difficult situation in which to live, but if this is where you are, God wants to redeem your spouse and be glorified in your marriage. In the meantime, the best marriages of this sort are the result of a Christian showing honor and respect, rather than belittling the unsaved spouse.

It is only natural that a lost person would not understand spiritual things. "The man without the Spirit does not accept the things that come from the Spirit of God, for they are foolishness to him, and he cannot understand them, because they are spiritually discerned" (1 Cor. 2:14). If you are an intercessor married to a lost spouse, please exercise great discretion. Don't overlook the difficulty your spouse may have with spiritual things. Honor and respect your loved one.

Intercessor, if you want your spouse to become a Christian, then be Christlike. Serve her graciously and respect her opinions about biblical issues, even if you feel she is misled. Exercise caution that you don't cause resentment by ignoring and neglecting her, especially by putting her down. Don't insist on being right when God has called the two of you to be one!

THE OTHER MAN

In a spiritual sense, there is another man in Alice's life, the Lord Jesus, and she deeply loves Him. I have had to learn to release her to Him and to His call upon her life. I would be less than candid if I didn't admit to you that at times I've experienced fleeting moments of jealousy—times when I found myself bothered that she would spend so much time so passionately involved with Him. If this has been a struggle for me, imagine what a lost husband or wife might feel.

If I did not know and love Jesus, too, this would be much more difficult for me. The protection of our marriage is that I love Him more than I love her, and she loves Him more than she loves me! Our love for Him keeps us faithful to our marriage vows.

If you are an intercessor married to a person without Christ, this puts a great deal of additional responsibility on you. Learn to exercise loving sensitivity to your spouse. Look for ways to pray while he is away at work—before he rises in the morning or after he retires at night. Imagine the dilemma of a lost man or woman married to one who passionately pursues Jesus. As one intercessor's lost husband confessed to me one day, "It would be hard enough to compete with 'the other man' I could see. How do I deal with this One that I can't see?"

WHEN YOUR SPOUSE COMES TO THE LORD

I would be remiss if I failed to mention this issue. An intercessor will cry, wail, travail, moan and complain to the Lord for their lost wife or husband, sometimes for years. The prayer warrior has the sympathy of the church, getting special attention in Sunday School and in prayer meetings over the issue of the lost spouse. But once the spouse comes to Christ, the intercessor drops out of church!

I've seen it happen over and over again. Why? What happens?

First, the intercessor's personal identity has become wrapped up in having a lost husband or wife. When the spouse is born again, the intercessor loses a part of her significance. She becomes awkward at church. All of her church relationships begin to change as her spouse gets involved.

Second, when the newly saved spouse begins to show signs of spiritual life and initiative, and begins to carry his own spiritual weight in the family, it is easy for the one who prayed all those years to begin to resent her spouse's newfound passion for the Lord. She becomes angry with God!

Intercessor, if you are going to fast and pray to see your spouse saved, you had better check your motives first. Are you going to bail out once he or she gets saved?

As a young evangelist, I was conducting a revival at First Baptist Church in Donaldsonville, Louisiana, in 1969. One afternoon I asked the pastor if I could make some evangelistic visits.

He said, "Yes, I have one old man here in his late seventies. He is dying of heart disease. His wife, a prayin' woman, has been a faithful member here for many years. But he is a hard, crusty case. He has no interest in the Lord at all."

"Fine," I said. "Sounds like just the kind of visit I'd enjoy making!"

Knocking on the screen door of the old, white wood-framed house I heard a feeble voice ask, "Who is it?"

"Mr. Johnson, my name is Eddie Smith. I'm coming in to talk with you."

Opening the door, I saw the sickly old man sitting in a rocking chair, smoking a cigar and drinking a can of beer. As usual I had no trouble getting to the point.

"Sir, the pastor at your wife's church told me you're dying. I wanted to come by and ask, if you were to die today, would you go to heaven?"

His answer shocked me.

"Young man," he began. "Don't you think religion should begin at home?"

"Certainly, sir." I replied.

"Well, so do I," he said. "I'm sure my wife asked you to come talk to me. For years she goes down to that church and gets with her friends and cries over me. Everybody feels sorry for her because I'm not a Christian. Then she comes home, treats me like hell and never takes care of this place. I just think religion should begin at home.

"To be honest with you, I think the worst thing that could happen to her would be for me to get religion. She'd no longer be the center of attention down there at her church."

PUBLIC EMBARRASSMENT

Sometimes immature intercessors will monopolize a corporate prayer meeting by praying too long or too often, thus taking up time that should be shared with others. Immature intercessors may also enter into travail or public prophecy at inappropriate times and places. (That which is biblical is not always appropriate.) The intercessor's spouse, whether lost or saved, can suffer embarrassment from an intercessor's insensitivity and lack of restraint at such times.

As an intercessor, always remember that your words and actions reflect on the one to whom you are married. Perhaps it's because I am a musician, but I have cringed compassionately for the spouses of a few intercessors who, though not musicians, have attempted to sing prophetically in public. Their painful performance made their spouses want to push a button and drop through the floor.

Intercessors, exercise sensitivity to your partners. You will reap many rewards as you love them deeply and represent them honorably for Christ's sake. Never put your spouse down in public, no matter how cute it might sound. If you want to share a humorous story or one that could cause your partner embarrassment, ask his permission first.

SUPERNATURALLY SPIRITUAL OR SUPERNATURALLY NATURAL?

God is looking for spiritual fruit, not religious nuts! It doesn't take a rocket scientist or an advanced theologian to figure out that the Holy Spirit doesn't make one "supernaturally spiritual" or "spiritually weird." After 27 years of working in deliverance, I have found that spiritual weirdness is usually the product of a religious spirit or demon. The Holy Spirit makes a person "supernaturally natural."

> God is looking for spiritual fruit,
> not religious nuts!

Intercessor, please hear me. If you are married to a lost person, all of your religious activity or spiritual idiosyncrasies will not draw your spouse toward Jesus. Jesus despises "religious stuff," and so does your lost spouse. Jesus was a supernaturally natural man. He was all God and all man. Yet, being all God, He was a friend of sinners (see Matt. 11:19). Lost people loved being around Him. Although the purity of His life undoubtedly challenged their worldliness, His personality and His presence must have been a joy to them. Being spiritually flaky is not being like Jesus!

I'll never forget sitting in a crowded Mexican food restaurant one summer Sunday in south Texas when our hostess began her "religious activity." Her three-year-old son was loose, running from table to table pulling on tablecloths, stealing silverware and generally wreaking havoc. All the while, his mother was oblivious to his rampage of destruction. With her eyes closed, her head heavenward and her hands held upward, she was chattering like a jungle monkey, "Oh Jesus, Jesus, Jesus. Oh hallelujah! Jesus, Jesus, Jesus."

Alice and I were embarrassed and humiliated in that restaurant. We were grieved over the appearance this woman was giving the waitress and busboys working near us. Intercessors, wake up! This kind of display doesn't impress us, your spouse or your friends; it depresses us. It isn't Christlike!

Some intercessors tend to be mystical. One might say they have become too heavenly minded to be any earthly good. Of course, that's impossible. The only earthly good any of us possesses is our commitment to put on the mind of Christ. What is usually meant by that phrase is not that a person is heavenly minded, but rather that they are spiritually weird!

AN INTERCESSOR'S PRIORITIES

Some male intercessors depend on their wives to support the family, because, they say, the ministry of intercession is their priority. Sir, you are not some shaved-head Tibetan monk wrapped in a bed sheet, perched atop Mount Everest humming a mantra. Your family and their well-being must always be your first priority.

In like manner, a woman who is an intercessor must first be a Christian, then a godly wife and mother, *then* minister outside the family. Her first ministry is to the family. She is responsible for her home ministry, as well as the other responsibilities God assigns to her. That is not to say that her family and husband can't and shouldn't help her in her work. I have tried to encourage Alice's ministry. I can do the laundry, grocery shopping or vacuuming, and I do so from time to time to help.

Any intercessor, male or female, should see to it that their family doesn't suffer the burdens they are called to bear. For example, intercessors tend to fast often. When he or she is fasting, the family should hardly notice it (see Matt. 16:16). The praying person shouldn't be irritable, cranky or self-centered, asking for pity or special considerations. If the intercessor whines or complains, "I wish I could eat, that's my favorite dish," it is a sign of spiritual immaturity. Intercessors, if you prepare a meal, then sit at the table with your family while they eat and enter pleasant conversation with them. Don't make others feel uncomfortable or unspiritual because they are not fasting with you. I admire the tenacity of intercessors who are diligent to fast and pray faithfully. How they do it, God only knows. He graces them, and they in turn grace us!

Of course, a spouse who is not fasting at the time should exercise the "golden rule." When one is fasting, the other can compensate by offering to cook or to take the kids out to eat. And try not to snack in front of your fasting partner.

FASTING FROM SEXUAL INTIMACY

If you are married to an intercessor or to a person who fasts and prays, there may be times when the two of you agree to refrain from sexual intimacy.

God says:

> The wife hath not power of her own body, but the husband: and likewise also the husband hath not power of his own body, but the wife. Defraud ye not one the other, except it be with consent for a time, that ye may give yourselves to fasting and prayer; and come together again, that Satan tempt you not for your incontinency (1 Cor. 7:4,5, KJV).

Please notice this abstinence is temporary. It says "for a time" and is specifically for seasons of prayer and fasting.

One of the most devastating things that can happen to a marriage is for one partner to unilaterally withhold sexual intimacy from the other indefinitely. It is selfish and wicked. God says it is to be "with consent." Both husband and wife agree to these temporary times of celibacy. If you are married to an unbeliever, give them advance notice that you are fasting from EVERY-THING! If they do not want to fast from sexual relations, do not deny them. The Lord knows your heart.

Back in the early '70s, we had friends who were in the ministry, yet were deceived concerning this issue. Alice received a call from her girlfriend, who tearfully expressed her concern. Supposedly God had told her husband that he was not to touch, kiss or to have sex with her for a period of two years because he was "set aside" for the ministry. This couldn't have been God's voice, because contrary to Scripture, this husband certainly did not have his wife's consent!

This spiritual deception occasionally snags intercessors. One female intercessor with whom Alice and I have counseled said that, while in her prayer closet, the Lord told her to remove her wedding rings. "You are not to wear them any longer," He supposedly instructed her. "You are married to me." Hello-o-o! Earth to intercessor! This was not the Lord! It was a demonic spirit, and it finally destroyed her marriage.

God does not tell us to do things that are contrary to His Word. But this particular woman wouldn't listen to counsel from any source. Convinced she had heard from God, she embraced the lies and isolated herself from the safety of the Body of Christ. The deception devastated her family. We were forced to watch helplessly as she ultimately lost a godly husband and a beautiful young son. What a tragic price to pay for spiritual pride and deception.

An intercessor from New York said the Lord told her to move from sleeping with her husband in the second-floor bedroom to sleeping in the basement, where her prayer room was located. She was instructed to sleep in her prayer room "with Jesus." Friend, this is demonic deception! Any voice that comes against the sacred union of your marriage is not God's voice. God will never undermine the foundation of your marriage. It is sacred to Him!

NIGHT WATCHES

Perhaps no more practical issue can trouble an intercessor's marriage than the issue of sleep or sleeplessness. God often shares His heart with intercessors, and for this reason they are quite visionary. It is almost like women's intuition. (Whose mother didn't have that? What's interesting is that male intercessors experience the same kind of intuition.) Praying people seem to sense what is going on "behind the scenes," even what is about to come to pass.

Countless nights I have rolled over to discover that Alice was not in bed, but in her closet with the Lord. Sometimes in quiet intimacy. Other times she's at war! It is common for Alice to spend a sleepless night over what she senses is happening to a friend or loved one. At times she feels certain she knows for whom or for what she is praying. Sometimes she hasn't a clue as to what is happening, only that it requires prayer. To those of us who are not intercessors, this can seem weird indeed! Having a sense that something is about to happen can cause the intercessor to be restless for no apparent reason.

Old Testament watchmen served three-hour watches relieved by turns (see Neh. 7:3). Intercessors typically have prayer watches to which God has assigned them. I often hear intercessors speak of their night watches. "On my bed I remember you; I think of you through the watches of the night" (Ps. 63:6).

A warning is in order here. There was the danger of watchmen sleeping on their posts, as referred to in Matthew 28:12-14 at the Resurrection. Understand, intercessors are never really off duty. They are on call 24 hours a day. "My eyes stay open through the watches of the night, that I may meditate on your promises" (Ps. 119:148).

Intercessors live somewhat unusual lives, many seeming to exist in their own individual time zones. Often an intercessor will complain of sleeplessness or insomnia. They say, "I can't seem to fall asleep," or "I awake suddenly in the night and have trouble going back to sleep." In the second case, the intercessor will often awaken at the same time each night (e.g., 3:33 A.M.).

The first time one of our intercessors asked me what he should do about insomnia, I was puzzled. "I don't know what to suggest," I replied. "Let me pray about it and seek the Lord, and I'll get back to you."

I went to the Word in search of his answer. What I found surprised even me. It appears that the quantity of sleep one gets does not seem to be that important to God. King David writes in the book of Psalms, "On his law he meditates day and night" (Ps. 1:2). Later, he says, "My tears have been my food day and night" (Ps. 42:3).

It probably isn't very encouraging to the intercessor in search of a good night's sleep to discover that, as far as God is concerned, sleeping is such a low priority. Jesus often prayed all night after ministering all day!

In the world of intercession there are actual night watches.

RESPONSE-ABILITY

These night watches are similar to watches I stood while in the U.S. Navy, where watches are scheduled around the clock for obvious security reasons. The "old ship Zion" has watches and watchmen as well—typically three-hour periods when God chooses to talk with His intercessors. Some are assigned the midnight to 3:00 A.M. watch; others stand the 3:00 to 6:00 A.M. watch. Jesus often prayed on the predawn watch (see Mark 1:35).

For many intercessors, their watches are seasonal. And, like the rotation of troops, intercessors tend to rotate through the different shifts. Intercessors report that they routinely find it difficult to sleep during these specific times. Amazingly, these warriors say that failure to sleep during their night watch causes them little or no fatigue the next day. They awake refreshed!

When our youngest daughter, Ashlee, was 10 years old, she experienced a three-week period during which she would awaken between midnight and 1:00 A.M. After a few nights, it occurred to us that this might be an issue of intercession rather than insomnia. God calls many children and uses them as powerful intercessors. It was in the night, you'll recall, that God spoke to the boy Samuel.

If you find yourself wide-awake at midnight or at 3:00 in the morning, it may be that God has assigned you to a night watch, a period of time for which He is holding you accountable! Arise and take your place as His watchman atop the wall for your family, your church, your city, your nation or whatever assignment He gives you.

If you don't know what the assignment is, then pray in general terms. You might pray like this: "Father, complete the work You have assigned to me for this time. Renew, save, restore, shield, break through, Lord! I stand before You to ask for Your mercy concerning the issue that is on Your heart."

Don't forget. You are only human. It may be that you will ascend to the place of prayer only to fall asleep in the process. Don't feel condemned by that. You were faithful to answer His call. And you are His beloved child. I believe that sometimes the Lord just wants to hold His sleeping child in His arms. He will awake us to see if we are willing to get up and stand watch. Our faithfulness to respond, or our "response-ability," is the key.

Too often we think of prayer as merely talking to God. We are also to enter His presence to hear what is on His heart. He who stands watch over you by night longs to commune with you atop the wall. Remember, Jesus is interceding for you (see Heb. 7:25). You don't stand watch for Him. You stand watch with Him!

6

Ten Pitfalls to Avoid

One morning, Charles, a young husband of an intercessor, came by my office seeking a word of counsel. "Pastor Eddie," he said, "I'm concerned. Last night I was sleeping soundly when I was suddenly awakened by an alarming slap across my chest. My wife bolted upright in bed and shrieked, 'Oh my God, Charles, wake up! We forgot to pray for the kids!' What's wrong with this?"

"Oh that's simple," I explained. "Your wife is superstitious. She looks at prayer like it's a lucky rabbit's foot or a horseshoe. She thinks your kids are safe because you pray for them."

"They're not?" he asked.

"Ours certainly aren't. Our kids are protected because we have given them to God. They are His property. Sure, we pray for our kids in order to come into agreement with Him for them. But their safety isn't dependent upon our prayers; it's dependent upon our God. If we should forget to pray, He won't forget our kids. He isn't limited in the least."

Religious superstition is just one potential trap that can ensnare Christians today. Intercessors and their spouses should be wary of at least ten other pitfalls that we have seen intercessors fall victim to in recent years.

1. Becoming Demon Conscious

The devil loves attention, and he's thrilled when he becomes the center of conversation. A demon-conscious intercessor is one who sees "a demon behind every bush."

One man was explaining to me how the devil had caused his car's transmission to fail. "When was the last time you serviced it?" I inquired.

"Serviced it? What do you mean?" he answered innocently.

If you fail to service your car or other mechanical device, it will fail, with or without a devil!

Many years ago, Alice hired a seamstress to make a dress for her. But before a stitch was sewn, a nervous seamstress called Alice.

"I can't sew this dress for you," she said.

"Why not?" Alice inquired.

"Because I took a magnifying glass to see the design on your gold buttons. There are lions on your buttons," the seamstress said.

"So?"

"They were growling at one another, so they must be of the devil. Like First Peter 5:8 says, 'The devil walks about like a roaring lion, seeking whom he may devour'" (*NKJV*).

This lady was acting out of superstition—Christian superstition.

Look, we live in a fallen world. Things break. Our job is to be good stewards over the things that God entrusts to us. It is a mistake to blame the works of our flesh (our lower nature) on the devil. Those things are our responsibility, and God will hold us, not Satan, accountable for them.

When we give the devil this kind of attention, he's got us just where he wants us.

2. Inflating the Importance of Satan

I recently invited an intercessor to be listed in the U.S. Prayer Directory, which we publish each year. "No way!" she exclaimed.

"Why wouldn't you want to be listed in the directory?" I inquired.

"Because," she said, "I don't want the devil to know where I live!"

Dryly, I chided, "Why, I'd be ashamed if the devil *didn't* know where I live."

Some intercessors—and far too many Christians—see Satan and God as almost equal beings, opposites who rule almost equal kingdoms. Nothing could be further from the truth!

Satan in no way compares to God—in power, in presence, in knowledge or anything else for that matter. God created him in righteousness. His sin and rebellion caused his fall. Satan exists only to serve the purposes of God. When God gets through with him, he will be put away forever!

Yes, he rebelled. However, he has already been judged, found guilty, disarmed, defeated and humiliated. We are now awaiting the final execution of his eternal death sentence.

3. Overspiritualizing Things

While it's true that many things—physical objects, words, numbers—in the natural world often have corresponding spiritual significance, some intercessors begin to believe that this is *always* the case. From condemning the practice of buying a tree at Christmas because some ancient persons worshiped trees, to wanting to move because their new zip code contains three sixes, these people are pushing reality to the outer limits. Such an intercessor has become superstitious and fearful.

Best-selling author and internationally known speaker Cindy

Jacobs describes "spiritually weird" people of prayer as "flaky intercessors." She writes that these men and women, who for a variety of reasons have drifted outside biblical guidelines in their zeal for prayer, pose a threat to the coming revival:

> They bring reproach on their ministries and confusion and division in the church. Flaky intercession could become a widespread problem in the '90s, for many prophetic voices are proclaiming that God is calling the church to intense prayer as a prelude to revival.
>
> Studies of past revivals indicate that they were birthed and bathed in prayer, but that the move of the Holy Spirit was short-circuited by the inability to sustain effective intercession. In many instances it was flaky intercession that undermined true prayer and destroyed revival.[1]

4. Soulishness

An undisciplined mind confuses soulishness and spirituality, allowing the soul to dominate the spirit. Some of what is referred to as "drunk in the Spirit" is nothing more than the intoxication of the soul.

Do I believe God can make one drunk in the Spirit? I do and I have seen it happen to those I know to have a deep walk with the Lord. But the spiritual dimension is so real to intercessors that they can easily fall prey to emotional foolishness if they fail to guard their hearts (see Prov. 4:23). Alice and I agree that this is how intercessors sometimes lose their credibility with church leadership.

5. False Travail

I have used the word "travail" a few times thus far to describe a physical and spiritual process an intercessor may undergo while in intense prayer. Perhaps I should explain this. Travailing prayer is a type of prayer that gives birth to something in the Spirit. It can be very intense, involving fervent prayer, tears, even groaning. Sometimes, however, what appears to be intercessory travail is not.

During a time of corporate intercession, an intercessor may begin to visualize and then strive to receive the burden of God that others are experiencing. But instead of genuine, God-assigned travail that flows from the spirit of the intercessor, a soulish "travail" is released through the mind and emotions, giving the intercessor a false experience.

Often the whole group stops praying to help someone give "spiritual birth." When one person becomes the center of attention, this is exactly what the enemy wants . . . total distraction! The enemy has effectively sidetracked the intercessors from the critical issue at hand—usually a prayer issue that Satan can't afford to leave unchallenged. The easiest way for him to get relief from focused, united prayer is to tantalize the group with a bizarre experience. Sadly, we have witnessed this all over the world in both evangelical and charismatic prayer circles.

6. Isolationism

The intercessor who falls into isolationism, or escapism, becomes a loner. Rather than the prayer closet being a holy place to meet God, it becomes a place in which to hide. It becomes a way the intercessor can escape from personal relationships and responsibilities with a "holy excuse." After all, how can anyone argue with the call of God on a person's life? And why would anyone be against prayer?

This misguided intercessor attempts to build the case that he or she can no longer keep house or hold a job. Other family members have to take up the slack and do double duty because the intercessor is committed to "higher" things. This is an expression of spiritual pride and often takes advantage of others, usually the ones who love them most. If you do this to a lost spouse, forget about him ever wanting to become a Christian!

7. Elitism, or Lack of Accountability to Brethren

Isolationism often leads to a lack of spiritual accountability. Holding to a martyr complex, the lone intercessor begins to feel that no one understands her. She translates this to mean: *I'm special.*

As a prayer elitist, she begins to withdraw, especially from strong Christians, and surround herself with those who are spiritually weaker than she. In the flesh, she can easily intimidate others with her forceful personality or her way with words. She can manipulate others with tears, moodiness or mysteries she feels she alone possesses. These are often controlling intercessors who would become spiritual gurus, or self-appointed ministers.

> Never submit to the
> spiritual leadership of anyone
> who is not submitted to the spiritual
> leadership of the local church.

Sometimes they seek undue attention from their pastors. Spiritual pride is evidenced when our need to be right is elevated above the need to be one. This results in crippled or stunted relationships. Such a person will sacrifice meaningful, loving relationships for nonessential issues and personal spiritual opinions.

Beware of this type of person. Never submit yourself to the spiritual leadership of anyone who is not submitted to the spiritual leadership of the local church. God has chosen from the beginning to work through His Church. Some think they need only be submitted to God, but this is not the biblical pattern. We find the principles of accountability even in the Old Testament. Moses was submitted to Jethro, his father-in-law. Joseph was accountable to Pharaoh. Deborah was answerable to Balak; Joshua to his commanders.

God has designed the Church so that the members are interdependent upon each other. Every one of us, pastors as well, should have the spiritual oversight and accountability of at least one other brother or sister in the Lord. Preferably this is a person with strength of character beyond our own to whom we will listen and submit.

8. Lack of Accountability to the Church

An intercessor who is not accountable to his or her brothers and sisters in Christ will gradually deny accountability to God's designated spiritual authority. This intercessor will begin to elevate personal revelation (what he or she feels God is saying now) above Scripture (what He has already said) and proclaim this to anyone who will listen.

DANGER! We are living at a time when these "prophetic renegades" are infiltrating the Church. They are divisive in the flock and disrespectful, even critical of pastors. They will destroy people's confidence in their pastors by portraying him as someone who simply isn't spiritual enough to understand the deep truths of God. Intercessors who operate in this deception surround themselves with others who are unhappy and have difficulty following pastoral leadership. Out of synch with the vision of the church, they may begin to have "private" meetings, which may result in unauthorized ministries. In this way, these unaccountable prayer warriors compete with the pastor for the allegiance of the people.

A good pastor doesn't compete with Jesus for the love of His Bride. He has no selfish desire for her affection, so it is difficult for the pastor to confront someone in the church who is vying for the church's affection. A confrontation can give the appearance that the pastor is jealous of the intercessor, rather than guarding the flock's devotion to her true lover and groom, the Lord Jesus.

9. Witchcraft Praying

Witchcraft prayer is the act of consciously praying contrary to God's revealed will and is characterized by the use of controlling or manipulative prayer.

Intercessors must exercise caution not to confuse their own will with God's will. When praying for family members, spouses, pastors or others, it is important that they limit prayers to the will of God. God's will, of course, is found in His Word. It is always safe to pray the Scriptures. But praying people should avoid praying their opinions and desires.

An example of witchcraft praying would be: "Lord, I pray that you'll straighten my pastor out! You know how blind and stubborn he is, God. Just break him if you have to." An implied curse, or hex, is in this prayer.

Alice and I call this "witchcraft prayer" because the very essence of witchcraft is control. Prayer based on a desire to control is essentially the practice of witchcraft. In pagan religions and in witchcraft, the grace and sovereignty of a biblical God are unknown. The practitioner is instead dealing with spiritual "forces" that must be appeased, bribed and otherwise manipulated.

But God cannot be manipulated, and He alone is to be in control. We must always pray His will. For example, "Father, I ask you to be gracious to my pastor today. Conform him to the image of your Son" (see Rom. 8:29).

This is praying in partnership with God (see 1 John 5:14,15). Nothing comes as close to praying His will as does praying the Scripture.

10. Ministering out of Hurt

Some intercessors have been wounded and even spiritually abused. Sadly, this abuse is sometimes at the hands of spiritual leadership who misunderstand and mistreat them.

Quite often the pastor isn't even aware of what is happening. Of course, it is also possible that the pastor feels threatened by an intercessor's spiritual gifts. The pastor, who should be equipping his budding prayer warriors and providing them a safe place to experiment and learn, may even confuse immaturity with impurity and "blow them away."

Rather than seek reconciliation, the intercessor may cling to resentment, resulting in a warped view of leadership. A wounded intercessor may refuse to see leaders as the fallen men or women that they are and offer no grace to the leaders. From this perspective, leaders are a threat rather than a blessing, and the intercessor is no longer able to submit to authority. Unaccountable and unprotected, the wounded intercessor is left exposed without godly spiritual cover.

This most often results in the following process:

1. The intercessor may lick her wounds, seek to become the center of attention and seek to manipulate others with self-pity.
2. Her spiritual pride now wounded, the intercessor adopts a martyr complex, elevating herself and her ideas above others, especially above those in authority.
3. The intercessor becomes critical of church authorities. Her spiritual gift of discernment, now being fleshly motivated rather than spiritually empowered, becomes judgmental.
4. The intercessor surrounds herself with other wounded, critical soldiers in order to justify her right to remain wounded and bitter!

All of these can be the result of ministering out of hurt—ministering from one's emotions, rather than out of one's spirit.

HOW TO PROTECT YOURSELF AND YOUR SPOUSE

When an intercessor falls into one or more of these traps, his or her effectiveness for God has been compromised. Unaware of the flaws at first, this person will eventually suffer a spiritual "melt-down." If you feel the Holy Spirit causing you to question leadership, submit your questions to those who are your spiritual cover, like your spouse or your pastor. Ask them to love you enough to tell you if they feel you are walking dangerously close to any of these snares.

You can find protection from these and other pitfalls in three ways:

- *Stay close to God.* Walk in holiness and purity and seek Him daily.
- *Stay close to the Word.* Every experience, every idea, every spiritual impression must be subject to the written Word of God. God will never say something contradictory to what He has written!
- *Stay close to one another.* Each Christian needs to have meaningful relationships with mature Christians. It is here that accountability is maintained.

Remember, accountability establishes your credibility.

Note
1. Cindy Jacobs, *Possessing the Gates of the Enemy* (Grand Rapids: Chosen Books, 1991), p. 126.

7

A Few Good Men

One night during the Revolutionary War, near a British camp not far from the Hudson, a Highland soldier was caught creeping stealthily back to his quarters out of the woods. He was taken before his commanding officer and charged with holding communication with the enemy.

The Highlander pleaded that he had gone into the woods to pray by himself; that was his only defense. The commanding officer was himself a Scot, and a Christian, but he had no sympathy for the culprit.

"Have you been in the habit, sir, of spending hours in private prayer?" he asked sternly.

"Yes, sir," was the reply.

"Then down on your knees and pray now!" roared the officer. "You never before had so much need of it."

Expecting immediate death, the soldier knelt and

poured out his soul in a prayer that, for aptness and simple expressive eloquence, could not have been inspired except by the power of the Holy Spirit.

"You may go," said the officer, when he had finished. "I believe your story. If you had not been often at drill, you could not have got on so well at review."[1]

PRAYING MEN OF THE BIBLE

The prayer closet is not off-limits to men! While it is true that women outnumber men among those who have identified and accepted the call of intercession today, it is not true that intercession is strictly the purview of women in the Church. Consider for a moment a few biblical examples of men who were powerful in prayer.

Ezekiel
We know Ezekiel was a prophet. But, have you pondered those instances where Ezekiel was functioning in the gift of an intercessor? "Cry and howl, son of man: for it shall be upon my people, it shall be upon all the princes of Israel " (Ezek. 21:12, *KJV*).

Moses
Moses was a great leader. We know him as a mighty deliverer, yet he was a powerful intercessor as well. In fact, he was so fervent in prayer that he risked his own life for the nation of Israel:

Now it came to pass on the next day that Moses said to the people, "You have committed a great sin. So now I will go up to the Lord; perhaps I can make atonement for your sin." Then Moses returned to the Lord and said, "Oh, these people have committed a great sin, and have made for themselves a god of gold! Yet now, if You will forgive their sin—but if not, I pray, blot me out of Your book which You have written" (Exod. 32:30-32).

Jeremiah

Jeremiah, "the weeping prophet," was a classic intercessor. In his book, Jeremiah mentions crying, weeping or wailing at least 48 times.

> Oh that my head were waters, and mine eyes a fountain of tears, that I might weep day and night for the slain of the daughter of my people! (Jer. 9:1, *KJV*).

> But if you will not hear it, my soul will weep in secret for your pride; my eyes will weep bitterly and run down with tears, because the Lord's flock has been taken captive (Jer. 13:17, *NKJV*).

Here is another example of a classic intercessory experience: "Therefore I will wail for Moab, and I will cry out for all Moab; I will mourn for the men of Kir Heres" (Jer. 48:31, *NKJV*).

Jesus

A casual reading of the Gospels reveals that prayer was a major activity in the life of Christ. Jesus prayed in gardens, on mountaintops, in deserts and in the Temple. He prayed before dawn, all night and for forty days at a time! It should come as no surprise to us that He now is committed to full-time intercession at the right hand of the Father (see Heb. 7:25).

Paul

We see the apostle Paul expressing the heart of an intercessor in Galatians 4:19: "My little children, of whom I travail in birth again until Christ be formed in you" (*KJV*). Paul wrote to the

Thessalonians, "For you remember, brethren, our labor and toil; for laboring night and day, that we might not be a burden to any of you, we preached to you the gospel of God" (1 Thess. 2:9, *NKJV*).

PRAYING MEN IN MODERN TIMES

In the last two centuries alone, God has raised up some outstanding male intercessors to serve His Church.

Andrew Murray

In his book *Revival Fire*, Wesley Duewel gives us a picture of the influence this man had on the people of his day:

> For some years Rev. Andrew Murray, Sr. longed and prayed for revival in South Africa. Every Friday night he spent several hours in prayer. The revivals of 1858 in the United States and 1859 in Northern Ireland were reported in the Dutch Reformed journals. A little book on *The Power of Prayer* was published. Individuals and prayer groups in various places across South Africa began to pray specifically for revival.
>
> In April 1860, a conference attended by 374 was convened at Worcester, South Africa. Representatives of twenty congregations (sixteen Dutch Reformed, plus Methodist and Presbyterian leaders) gathered. The main topic was revival. Andrew Murray, Sr. was moved to tears and had to stop speaking. His son, Andrew Murray, Jr., prayed with such power that some say the conference marked the beginning of the revival.
>
> Fifty days after the Worcester conference, revival fires began to burn. In Montague, near Worcester, a prayer revival began in the Methodist church. Prayer meetings were held every night and on Monday, Wednesday and

Friday mornings, sometimes as early as 3:00 A.M. People who had never prayed before began to pray.

One evening God anointed a young girl to pray. Young and old began to cry to God for mercy and continued until midnight. As Dutch Reformed people left their prayer meetings, they crowded into the Methodist church. For weeks the village of Montague experienced great conviction of sin. Strong men cried to God in anguish. Six prayer meetings were going on throughout the village. The report reached Worcester, and prayer meetings began there as well. Whole families, both European and native African, were humbled before God.[2]

Rees Howells

A radical intercessor, this Welshman who lived in the early 1900s experienced revival fire in Wales and led many intercessors into intense, concentrated prayer for the specific purpose of changing the course of World War II:

> During the four years previous to the outbreak of World War II . . . the Lord was changing the burden on Mr. Howells from local concerns . . . to national and international affairs. As he said, "The world became our parish and we were led to be responsible to intercede for countries and nations."
>
> It was in March 1936 that Mr. Howells began to see clearly that Hitler was Satan's agent for preventing the gospel going to every creature. As he said later, "In fighting Hitler we have always said that we were not up against man, but the devil. Mussolini is a man, but Hitler is different. He can tell the day this 'spirit' came into him."[3]

Cindy Jacobs, in her book *Possessing the Gates of the Enemy,* quotes this powerful prayer warrior as saying, "The intercession of the Holy Ghost for the saints in this present evil world must be made through believers filled with the Holy Ghost."[4]

George Mueller

A great intercessor, George Mueller possessed the gift of faith to feed the mouths of hundreds of orphans and see the salvation of multitudes. Dutch Sheets describes his persistence in the book *Intercessory Prayer:*

> [Mueller said] "The great point is never to give up until the answer comes. I have been praying for sixty-three years and eight months for one man's conversion. He is not saved yet, but he will be. How can it be otherwise . . . I am praying." The day came when Mueller's friend received Christ. It did not come until Mueller's casket was lowered in the ground. There, near an open grave, this friend gave his heart to God. Prayers of perseverance had won another battle. Mueller's success may be summarized in four powerful words: He did not quit.[5]

YOU CAN'T KEEP 'EM DOWN ON THE FARM

Most biographies of famous intercessors have been written about men. With few exceptions—most notably accounts of the work of Madame Guyon and Jessie Pen Lewis—not many books record the lives and ministries of women intercessors. Women were undoubtedly intercessors in previous generations, but until the last hundred years, few women were given public forums. Not surprisingly, women in all forms of ministry were relegated to serving God in relative obscurity.

However, in the last 150 years fewer men have been available for

the ministry of intercession. With the advent of the industrial revolution, men became preoccupied with business, leaving their farms
for the factory. In so doing, they also left their stumps, woodsheds,
tractors or whatever had served as their "prayer closets."

No longer working on family farms attached to their resi-
dences, increasing numbers of men worked in offices and facto-
ries far from home. Their time and privacy were reduced.
Competition, success in business and accumulation of wealth
became lifelong pursuits.

Simultaneously, the Church began to imitate the business
community. In many cases, the *business* of doing church took
precedence over the *ministry* of being the Church. The word
"board," for example, was coined by the secular business community and later adopted by churches supervised by a board of
deacons.

> Revival is our only hope for survival.
> Revival means nothing less
> than God's presence.

Sadly, spiritual men began to be measured by their achieve-
ments, their acumen and their articulate manner, rather than by
their willingness to access God's presence and procure His
power. They became known for their ability to get things done,
rather than their commitment to seek God's intervention.

Men began to see prayer as less than vital to the success of the
Church, much less vital to her survival! The Church became
everything *but* a house of prayer. Churches became houses of
sports, musical productions, preaching.

Even after years of dreaming, scheming, and implementing
plan after plan, when things weren't going well for the Church,
its leaders held out hope for a new and better man to produce
a new and better plan.

Today, wise and experienced pastors no longer believe that man will come up with the solutions to meet the Church's needs. They know that revival is our only hope for survival. Revival means nothing less than God's presence, God's intervention in the affairs of man.

WOMEN ANSWER THE CALL

Thankfully, during the past 150 years, women have taken up the slack with regard to the ministry of intercession. After all, intercession required little public attention. Women were uniquely qualified. They had a natural sensitivity to the Lord and to the needs of others, as well as a willingness to selflessly bear the burdens of others.

The faithfulness of God's women to pray has kept the Church afloat and has resulted in increased opportunity, responsibility and visibility for women in ministry today. Women such as Vonette Bright, Kay Arthur, Evelyn Christenson, Mary Lance Sisk, Cindy Jacobs, Bobbye Byerly, Alice Smith and thousands of other godly women have helped forge the historic worldwide prayer movement we are experiencing today. And, in almost every nation, in almost every segment of the Church, women are becoming more equitable partners with men in public ministry.

It is also widely believed that women are largely responsible for ushering in—through prayer—the current renewal and revival movement, especially among men as evidenced by men's ministries like Promise Keepers.

MEN ARE RETURNING TO PRAYER

Again, intercession is not an exclusively feminine ministry. While it is true that we have far too few contemporary male intercessory role models and mentors, we are now seeing God restore gender balance to this important ministry. Men and women are now bringing their respective God-given abilities and qualities to the work of intercessory prayer in greater numbers than ever before.

Men, who in years past have exercised the greater influence upon Church leadership, are recognizing and accepting their call to intercession. Therefore, leadership is becoming more aware of the ministry of intercession. Pastors are increasingly ready to identify and employ intercessors in the work of the Church. They are understanding more and more the need for strong personal prayer support and for a solid prayer foundation for the Church's other ministries.

This revival of intercession, particularly among men, has provided us a growing list of male role models. Among them is Larry Lea, who in the 1980s challenged Christians to pray an hour each day using the model prayer Jesus gave His disciples.

Dick Eastman, president of Every Home for Christ, provides Christians with many tools for prayer. As a gifted intercessor, Dick knows how to tap into the heart of the average intercessor.

David Bryant, founder of Concerts of Prayer, International, has risen to prominence in the last twenty years by challenging the Church to engage in powerful corporate prayer.

Chuck Pierce, a strong prophetic intercessor and Executive Director of the World Prayer Center in Colorado Springs, leads dozens of conferences each year, training thousands of intercessors.

John Dawson, whose mother Joy Dawson is a leading intercessor, has become the internationally recognized leader in reconciliation.

Steve Hawthorne, a highly trained and experienced intercessor, has become a world leader in the practice of prayerwalking.

Southern Baptist prayer leader Henry Blackaby is being used of God across denominational lines and on every continent to challenge the Church to do only what we see the Father doing.

Fuller Seminary professor C. Peter Wagner, like no other

person, has equipped the international prayer movement with dozens of best-selling books and resources.

At an age when most men begin looking at retirement, Campus Crusade for Christ founder Bill Bright has taken an assignment from the Lord to mobilize two million North American Christians who will fast and pray for 40 days by year-end 2000.

Jim Goll tells a story of my friend Dick Simmons, a personal intercessor who mobilizes men to pray:

> More than 30 years ago, Dick was attending Bible college in New York City. He was marked for intercession. In the middle of the night on the bank of the Hudson River, he began to cry out to the Lord in intercession for New York City. He prayed at the top of his lungs, "Lord, I beseech Thee that You send forth laborers unto Your field!" His agonized prayers were so loud at 2:00 A.M. (even by New York City standards!) that he suddenly was bathed in floodlights on the riverbank.
>
> Cautious police officers shouted out, "What are you doing? You have been reported for disturbing the peace because you've been waking up people!"
>
> Dick bellowed back, "Oh, I am just praying to the Lord of the harvest that He would send forth laborers into His field."
>
> The police officers must have been shocked, or else they agreed with Brother Simmons. They let him go without any charges or warning. That very night, the Holy Spirit of God descended on a little skinny preacher in rural Pennsylvania and gave him a divine call to take the gospel to New York City. Do you know his name? It was David Wilkerson.
>
> It is no wonder that when David Wilkerson established the first Teen Challenge Center in New York City, he chose Dick Simmons to be its first director.[6]

UNSUNG HEROES

Of course, many lesser-known men are also providing effective leadership in the ministry of intercession. Some are being used in the privacy of their own prayer closets. Others are being used of God to coordinate prayer and prayer ministries.

One such man is Charles Doolittle of Camarillo, California, who is prayer coordinator of his local church. Charles is a police officer, a physically towering man trained in hand-to-hand combat. Yet this gentle giant is also a highly trained spiritual warrior.

In cities across America, God has raised up city prayer coordinators. Some are men like Jean-Claude Chevalmé in Las Vegas, Nevada, and Lee Rushing in Big Spring, Texas. Elsewhere, men and women are teaming to do the job. Hal and Cheryl Sacks in Phoenix, Arizona, and Barney Fields and Laurie Huffman in El Paso, Texas, are good examples.

Most major cities now have prayer networks that cry out to the Lord for citywide revival. Some coordinate prayer for regions like Lynn Heatley and Norm Brinkley in California. God is using the U.S. Prayer Track's Tim James and his wife, Joyce, to disciple intercessors across America. Strategic national prayer leaders include Alvin Vander Griend with the Denominational Prayer Leaders Network, Steve Shanklin with Promise Keepers and Chicago's Phil Miglioratti, founder of the National Pastor's Prayer Network.

The bottom line is this: Men are joining the ranks of intercessors and prayer mobilizers in record numbers. Once again, men are a vital part of what God is doing through prayer on the earth in this desperate hour.

God works because of prayer! Angels minister as a result of prayer. This current historic prayer movement seems to be just beginning. Moreover, there are already signs of revival on the horizon.

Yes, if you are married to a man who is an intercessor, your husband is a precious gift to the Church, to you and to your family.

Notes

1. A. Bernard Webber, *Choice Illustrations* (Grand Rapids: Zondervan Publishing House), p. 94.
2. Wesley Duewel, *Revival Fire* (Grand Rapids: Zondervan Publishing House, 1995), p. 172.
3. Norman Grubb, *Rees Howells, Intercessor* (Fort Washington, Pennsylvania: Christian Literature Crusade), p. 246.
4. Cindy Jacobs, *Possessing the Gates of the Enemy* (Grand Rapids: Chosen Books, 1991), p. 30.
5. Dutch Sheets, *Intercessory Prayer* (Ventura: Regal Books, 1997), p. 197.
6. Jim Goll, *The Lost Art of Intercession* (Shippensburg, PA: Destiny Image, 1997), p. 100.

8

Help! My Husband Is an Intercessor

Chuck Pierce, director of the World Prayer Center in Colorado Springs, is on the cutting edge as a prophetic intercessor. He says that one night while he was in deep intercession his wife, Pam, the mother of their five children, came in and announced, "If you could pull yourself down out of the heavenlies for a few minutes and lend a hand with this dirty laundry, I'd certainly appreciate it."

I admit, there has been a time or two in almost three decades of marriage that I have been tempted to make a similar pronouncement.

First, let me congratulate you women who are married to intercessors. Of all the ministries to which a man could be called, none is more important than the ministry of intercessory prayer. Alice's prayer for our family is more important to us than any other thing she could provide for us. Thank God for men who are committed to intercede for the needs of others, for revival and for spiritual awakening in our world! These men give their families the priceless gift of prayer. However, in all honesty, living with such men also presents its share of challenges.

"HE'S TOO EMOTIONAL"

Communication can be difficult at times, even in the best of marriages. As more and more men discover God's intercessory call on their lives, I am spending more time counseling on this issue with women whose husbands are intercessors. They find that just understanding their husbands can be quite a challenge.

"He's too emotional," the wives of male intercessors sometimes complain. They are concerned that their husbands are too often tearful, weepy or burdened, many times for no apparent reason. Even the men themselves worry that they may be too emotional or appear weak. Some male intercessors don't understand intercessory travail and therefore resist the assignment when it comes upon them.

Men have a natural inclination to present a strong male image to their families. They feel it's important to the family's sense of security. It's that macho thing, you know.

It is said that when a young Muhammad Ali, then known as Cassius Clay, was at the height of his boxing career, he had a run-in with a stewardess as he boarded an airplane. The flight attendant requested, "Sir, please fasten your seat belt."

Clay is said to have quipped, "Ma'am, Superman don't need no seat belt."

To which the stewardess answered, "Sir, Superman don't need no airplane!" Thank God, He's not looking for supermen, or superwomen for that matter.

TOOLS OF THE TRADE

A posture of weakness before the Lord will make any intercessor effective. This contrast of being strong before one's family while being weak before the Throne is difficult for some men. The husband of one of our closest friends is an intercessor. For some time, he and his wife were both perplexed by what seemed to be his emotional instability. He was apt to break into tears at the most inopportune moments. His tender heart had become an embarrassment to him and his wife.

I explained to them that just as an auto mechanic must have his wrenches, tears are the tools of an intercessor's trade. As Dottie Rambo's song title says, "Tears are a language God understands." Consider the verse, "He that goeth forth and weepeth, bearing precious seed, shall doubtless come again with rejoicing, bringing his sheaves with him" (Ps. 126:6, *KJV*). When tears have watered the soil in which the seeds of prayer have been planted, we should expect a harvest!

A male intercessor, diagnosed by his doctor as manic-depressive, asked me to go with him to see his Christian psychiatrist. We explained to the psychiatrist some of the characteristic issues relating to the ministry of intercession. After we presented the psychiatrist with some biblical examples of men called to a ministry of intercession, the doctor removed his diagnosis from the man's chart!

This is not to say that clinical depression does not exist, but rather to say that we should be careful about building our boxes and shoving people into them.

PROVIDING FOR THE FAMILY

Male intercessors, like female intercessors, are often preoccupied with spiritual things. Gifted intercessors can seem to always be stuck in the prayer room, if not physically, then mentally. At times the male prayer warrior may seem out of touch with reality, and so committed to prayer that he ignores the everyday needs of his family.

In extreme cases, men refuse to hold a job or provide for their family, using their call to intercessory prayer as an excuse. Paul wrote that a man who fails to provide for his family is "worse than an infidel" (1 Tim. 5:8, *KJV*). If God actually calls someone to pray instead of hold an outside job, God's provision for his family will be the evidence. His wife won't have to support him. In other words, God's provision usually confirms God's direction.

In the fall of 1989, when God told Alice to quit working and spend her days in prayer, we were concerned how this move would affect us financially. One of our personal intercessors reported that God had told him in prayer that we were coming into a large amount of money. Sure enough, God miraculously provided Alice with $22,000 in real estate referral income during the next year—without her holding down a job! It was a blessed confirmation that she had heard from God.

> With a tough-guy, no-nonsense,
> John Wayne mentality,
> male intercessors can often overlook
> the fact that, at best,
> they see through a glass darkly.

A godly man knows that his spiritual responsibilities do not release him from his physical responsibilities. If a woman has an irresponsible husband, she has the unenviable task of balancing her role as helpmeet without further enabling his irresponsibility.

WAITING ON THE LORD

Christians often wrongly assume that intercession is a measure of maturity. It isn't. Intercession is an assignment from the Lord like any other. Many people of prayer are new, even immature Christians. In their immaturity, the inexperienced may use intercession as a way to get personal attention and affirmation from others. These "newbies" need to be equipped and guided to spiritual maturity.

New male intercessors, in particular, are often impulsive. They get "a word from God" and act on it immediately. To assume they have heard God clearly, correctly interpreted what they have heard and are applying it in the right way, is highly presumptuous! With that tough-guy, no-nonsense, John Wayne mentality, they overlook the fact that, at best, we prophesy in part, seeing through a glass darkly (see 1 Cor. 13:9,12).

Refusing to wait on the Lord to confirm the word, or to wait for their wives to come into agreement will breed marital resentment. Husbands, it is crucial that you allow your wives time to process and participate in important decisions. What is important to your wife? Contrary to what many have been taught, Ephesians 5:21 says, "Submit to one another." Intercessors, too, must reciprocally submit to their wives.

MY TEACHING GETS PUT TO THE TEST

God rarely allows me to teach something I have not personally experienced. If I have not already experienced the teaching, God in His infinite grace and wisdom soon allows me to do so!

In 1979, our family was living comfortably on a beautiful lake in north Texas. We had built a nice house, and the occasional revival or concert paid the bills. Only nine months after moving into our new home, I was offered a job in Houston as the executive director of an evangelistic association. My job would involve setting up area-wide evangelistic crusades, and I would have the opportunity to help produce a weekly, nationally broadcast Christian television program.

Returning home from the interview in Houston, my mind was racing. I was already mentally decorating my new office and planning my schedule for the next six months. As I drove north along the highway, I leaned over to Alice, looking for a bit of support and camaraderie. I said smugly, "Well, what do you think about the new job?"

She said rather sternly, "I really don't think that you are supposed to do this."

Dumbstruck with disbelief, I thought to myself, *Why, I was born for this job! This is a remarkable opportunity.* Continuing the argument by myself, it didn't take long for me to figure out that Alice and I were not on the same page. We weren't even in the same book! What is a husband or wife to do in this situation?

Admittedly, I don't have the gift of prophecy, nor am I the son of a prophet, and yet my intuition said, *Go!* Can you imagine the struggle that a male intercessor—especially one with the gift of prophecy—might face having to restrain his actions, when he feels so strongly God has spoken?

Male intercessors must guard against an elitist spirit that ignores their spouses' spiritual gifts or their spouses' ability to hear God's voice. If men don't exercise sensitivity in this area, their wives will eventually develop a defensive attitude that could prevent them from ever opening up to their husbands again.

"Honey," I whispered sweetly, "I really believe that the Lord is calling us to this new position. It certainly fits what God has equipped me to do. The pay and benefits are good. I just don't feel we are to pass this up. However, it's clear to me that you disagree. So here's what I'm going to do. First, tomorrow I will call the ministry in Houston and explain to them that we are unable to accept the job at this time, and more prayer is needed for us to come to a decision.

"Second, I will not mention this offer to you again. I'm not going to 'bug' you with this. Finally, I'm going to trust this whole thing to the Lord. If God has spoken to me, He can just as easily communicate it to you. If and when He does, you let me know."

Understand, I knew that I could be wrong. Perhaps it *wasn't* God's will. When I've taken time to consider Alice's input, God has often used her to keep me from stupid mistakes. But what if, while waiting for Alice, someone else got the job and I missed God's plan for my life? Was I confident in God's ability to speak to my wife? Could I leave the issue in His hands until He had finished working out all the details? It doesn't take much of a man to win an argument or walk all over his wife's feelings. But it takes quite a man to trust God!

Late one night, about six months later, Alice came into my study wiping tears from her eyes. "Eddie," she said, "The Lord has told me that you are to take that job in Houston."

"Oh Alice, I'm certain that the job was taken by someone else long ago."

"No, the Lord told me that it's there for you. Call them tomorrow and you'll see."

Amazingly, the job had not been taken by anyone else. Further, they explained that the night before, at the same time Alice had heard from the Lord, they were in prayer asking God to confirm His will in our hearts.

I accepted the job offer and we moved. The pay, the housing, literally everything about the job was better because we had waited those six months! That experience taught me that Alice and I can submit to each other in the fear of the Lord because we have a faithful God.

LAYING DOWN HIS LIFE FOR HIS WIFE

I received a call from a brokenhearted pastor, whose wife had for years resisted his call to the ministry. She had also been miserable living in the city where they resided. Undaunted by her resistance and unmoved by her feelings, this husband had forged ahead and continued to pastor his church. He was so committed to the ministry that it had been five years since he and his family had taken a vacation.

Without warning, his wife left him and moved to a distant city. She called to say she was through with the marriage. She was filing for divorce.

"What am I to do?" the pastor asked me tearfully.

"That's simple," I said. "You are to resign from your church and go to your wife. Repent to her for putting your ministry to others before your ministry to her. Convince her once and for all that she is your first earthly consideration."

"But I don't have the money to move," he said.

"Then you'll have to trust God."

After I prayed with this distraught pastor, he hung up to call his wife. A few minutes later he called me back. Joy had replaced his sorrow. "Eddie," he said, "You'll never guess what just happened! I called my wife and told her I am resigning the church this week and moving to be with her. I told her she was my first concern. As we talked, we were interrupted by call-waiting. Normally I would have ignored it, but somehow I felt it was important that I answer it. Eddie, it was an oil company calling to offer me $100 per acre for the mineral rights to 40 acres of land that I own. They are sending me a check for $4,000. God has instantly provided for my move!"

I believe that a man, intercessor or not, who honors his wife by laying down his life for her as this pastor is doing, will in time be ushered into God's perfect will for his life. None of us in the midst of Joseph's troubles would have believed that being sold into slavery in Egypt could be God's chosen route to greatness. I have no doubt that in the days ahead, through this pastor's move to be with his wife, they will be led into the center of God's will.

You might ask, *What about the church he is being forced to leave?* That church and their future are God's business. We can trust Him with that, too.

RELEASING YOUR HUSBAND TO INTERCESSION

Wives sometimes ask, "How do I release my husband to his intercessory ministry?" Here are a few tips:

Avoid the urge to criticize him. You should avoid the urge to judge or criticize your husband. Intercession is a difficult job. It's a heavy responsibility to present life-and-death issues before God's throne. Don't become an additional burden for him. Be a help, not a hindrance.

Listen to him. There are times when a prayer burden is so heavy your intercessor husband may just need you to listen as he ponders his approach to praying for the issue. He probably isn't looking for an answer; he may just need to vent.

Assist him. Perhaps you can offer to assist with the administration of the family. Again, I'm not suggesting that you take the place of your husband. Nevertheless, there may be ways you can help him when you sense he is under a particular spiritual burden or when he is fasting.

Guard your heart against jealousy. Guard against becoming jealous of his relationship with Christ. It's easy to feel ignored by your husband, especially if you don't experience the same level of intimacy with Christ that your husband shares in intercession. Pursue your own intimate relationship with Christ. Find your own rhythm of prayer. After all, intimacy with Christ is a journey, not a destination. Learn to accept yourself and where you are on the journey.

Release him to learn. Allow him to take advantage of opportunities to learn from other intercessors and teachers. Conferences, seminars and books offer a wealth of necessary training for him. Please consider the fact that your generosity to allow your spouse the time to learn from others during a season of training will have Kingdom effects. Remember, the fruit of your husband's prayers and tears in transforming lives will be applied to your heavenly account as well. Why? Because you partnered with him so he could be a more effective minister of intercession. The benefits are heavenly!

9

Honk if You Love Intercessors!

Pastors in record numbers are abandoning their mental caricatures of each other, forsaking suspicion and competition and developing meaningful relationships and strategic ministry partnerships. Pastors' prayer groups and prayer summits are proliferating as a growing number of pastors acknowledge the importance of prayer.

Spiritual leaders in our cities are identifying their intercessors, seeking to understand them and their unique ministry and establishing ministry partnerships with them. This partnership between the watchmen (intercessors) and gatekeepers (pastors) is God's latest move against the forces of darkness.

BORN FOR BATTLE

Around the world, God is bringing the ministries of the watchmen and the gatekeepers together in interdependent, blended ministry. In so doing, He has created a new awareness among His people that doing Church is a spiritual business that requires spiritual tools.

The army of Christ's spiritual kingdom is battling against real, spiritual enemies. We can no longer risk flying blind. The stakes are too high! During the Persian Gulf War, we saw on television the effectiveness of "night vision" infrared technology. Just as the infrared technology of Desert Storm allowed soldiers to see in the dark, prophetic intercessors can see in the spirit. Their spiritual sight, when developed and properly applied, is critical equipment for the war that lies ahead of us.

Just as Old Testament kings relied on their prophets, those uniquely "tuned" to hear God's voice, God has given pastors intercessors to be their ministry partners. Pastors need to employ these prayer warriors effectively in the days ahead to wage war against Satan.

Intercessors prayed Peter out of jail. A prophetic intercessor forewarned Paul of the dangers he would face in Jerusalem. James, one of three pillars of the Jerusalem church, may have died prematurely because the church did not pray for his protection.

Intercessors can sense dangers on the horizon, but when ignored by leadership, they can become very frustrated. Frustration can produce negativity. Then prayer warriors become part of the problem, not part of the solution.

Pastors must learn that intercessors will either war alongside you, or they will war without you. Intercessors were born for battle! When you find yourself in the trenches with bullets whizzing past your head—and you will—these same warriors will be there to fight with you . . . if you let them.

PASTORS WITHOUT PARTNERS

Although many pastors have a ministry of personal intercession, most pastors do not. Many pastors are committed to personal prayer, but intercession is not their primary call. Therefore, they may not understand intercession or intercessors.

After teaching at a seminar in San Jose, California, Alice and I were approached by a wonderful pastor in his seventies. Tearfully he said, "I have been a pastor more than forty years. Until today, I had no idea there were people in my church who actually love to pray."

A great deal of my time is spent consulting with pastors about their prayer ministries and their intercessors. Alice and I often teach intercessors how to understand and support their pastors. We find that in many cases pastors and intercessors tend to frustrate one another.

Understand this: The pastor-intercessor relationship will constantly be under assault. The enemy knows that unity empowers ministry (see Matt. 18:19). He also knows the significance of this partnership, and he cannot afford to ignore it. Neither can we!

Many years ago, my father left the local pastorate to become Southern Baptist Director of Missions in the Rio Grande Valley of south Texas. When I asked him what he missed most about being a pastor, my dad said, "Son, I miss my deacons." Dad was accustomed to having meaningful, fulfilling relationships with godly men. These relationships provided him with love, accountability, counsel and support.

Now that I am no longer the pastor of a church, I can understand his sentiments. I, too, miss the Thursday morning breakfasts with the elders and those monthly breakfasts with the elders and deacons. But most of all, I miss my intercessors.

Alice and I still try to maintain a close relationship with our intercessors. We regularly send them a letter and our speaking schedule, occasionally inviting them to our house for food, fellowship and prayer. The fact that I have written this book should serve as evidence of my love for intercessors. Allow me to express a few of the reasons why I love and appreciate these special people.

INTERCESSORS ARE PEOPLE OF PURPOSE

Overhearing a man describing another as one who does more for the Lord by accident than most people do on purpose, I responded, "No, the truth is that he does more on purpose than most people do on purpose!" That's one thing I love about intercessors: They are people of purpose!

A lively conversation developed when I asked a pastor friend the purpose of his church. Without thought he gave me a pat answer. "We're here to reach this community for Christ," he said. After a bit more discussion, it was clear that he didn't have a concrete plan to do so. In fact, he was having hardly any success at all. Someone has said that a vision without a mission will produce a visionary. But a vision with a mission will produce a missionary!

I love intercessors because they are people of purpose empowered by prayer. They know why they are here. Their desire to see revival in the Church and salvation for the lost drives these radical warriors to their knees! Intercessors have a vision *and* a mission. They are truly missionaries.

Prayer warriors know the truth about the clashing kingdoms of God and the devil. They take seriously Psalm 24:1, which says, "The earth is the Lord's, and all its fullness, the world and those who dwell therein" (*NKJV*). In the Garden of Eden, God gave rulership of the earth to man, who forfeited it to Satan through sin. The god of this world has usurped the rule of God through man (see 2 Cor. 4:4). Now, as a "squatter," the devil illegally claims ownership of the earth and its inhabitants.

But intercessors know that Christ has defeated and disarmed Satan and has been made Lord over all things (see Col. 2:15). These heavenly enforcers see themselves today in the "mopping up" stage of declaring and enforcing Christ's victory at Calvary. The average church member has little understanding of these spiritual truths. These truths, however, are part of an intercessor's basic training.

Prayer warriors take their job seriously, knowing that the future is being shaped today by prayer! They are the ones who ask. We all believe in prayer, but we don't all pray. I like intercessors because they ask, and when they ask, they believe (see Luke 11:9-13).

They are persistent, not quitters. Fully aware that this war is for souls, and commitment is required to win it, they have counted the cost and will gladly lay down their lives in the prayer closet. They not only ask, but they keep asking! Jesus promised that those who would keep asking would keep receiving (see Luke 18:1-8).

People of prayer typically have a heart-hunger for an intimate relationship with Christ. Intimacy with the Lord is central to both worship and intercession. Like King David, intercessors are worshipers as well as warriors.

Intercessors are fearless and unafraid to obey God. Intercessors are excitable. (Remember, one excited flea can bother a whole dog!) Adventurous, thriving on challenges, most are invigorating to be around. Risk-takers? Yes! And God is always showing up and doing amazing things in their lives. I'd rather be among a group of intercessors than with just about anybody.

Don't get me wrong. Intercessors don't necessarily come full-grown. They need instruction. But these unique people are powerful weapons in the arsenal of the Church. I used to tell our intercessors, "None of us are important, but all of us are necessary!"

And these burden-bearers are loyal. That's another reason I love them. They are loyal to God, always staying receptive to Him and His purposes. They are also loyal and sympathetic to the needs of others.

PASTORS BENEFIT FROM INTERCESSORS

Intercessors can be a challenge for any pastor. They tend to be the racehorses of the Church. (I don't think they'll object to that description.) Anyone can pastor plowhorses or riding ponies. But racehorses are high-strung and always set to go. At times it can be a challenge just to keep up with them.

> Intercessors, like racehorses, are often high-strung and always set to go. At times it can be a challenge just to keep up with them.

Years ago I attended a Christian broadcasters' convention in Washington, D.C. President Ronald Reagan was scheduled to speak to us in the afternoon. Men in dark suits with tiny earphones were stationed everywhere. Standing atop buildings, in the streets, walking the hallways and stairwells and riding the elevators, their presence was impressive. Dramatic tension built as we awaited the president's arrival.

When the president was twenty minutes overdue, the nervous, somewhat impatient crowd spontaneously began to sing hymns to pass the time. This was before the worship awakening our nation has experienced in recent years. Most of us were singing for the fun of it, harmonizing, enjoying ourselves and killing time.

Suddenly the doors of the auditorium swung open and a rush of dark-suited men covered the front of the auditorium like ants. Their chins were set, their teeth clenched. Each Secret Service agent continuously scoured the audience for potential threats to the president's safety.

We were singing "The King Is Coming" when, moments later, President Reagan burst through the double doors and strode confidently to the rostrum. The room was electric for the next twenty minutes as he articulately addressed the crowd. Then he turned and left as thunderous applause rattled the room. However, I was not as impressed with him as I was with his security. The Secret Service agents never flinched nor lost their focus.

If you are a pastor, God has provided intercessors to be a spiritual security force for you, your family and your church. These focused, fervent pray-ers are ready to provide "prayer cover" for you if you are willing. Peter Wagner calls them a "prayer shield." Assigned by God, intercessors are positioned to cover and sometimes forewarn you. They will often hear from God something that confirms what He has been saying to you.

CONGREGATIONS BENEFIT FROM INTERCESSORS

Many intercessors have pastoral gifts and are mercifully moved by the needs of others in their congregations. They are not only passionate about prayer, but compassionate for people. Supporting the congregation as they pray, these throne-room specialists believe God for healing, miracles, jobs and security.

Boosted by the Spirit, they are prayer pacesetters for the congregation. Their example reminds the Body of the importance of prayer. Because of their familiarity with and favor before the Throne, intercessors can be very helpful in corporate prayer meetings in helping to set the pace, the tone and the focus of group prayer.

Praying people can discern the heart of God and help find the direction for each corporate prayer meeting. The intercessor's zeal to pray and boldness to approach the Throne sets an example with his or her fervent passion for God and dependence upon Him (see Heb. 4:16; 10:19-22).

FAMILY MEMBERS BENEFIT FROM INTERCESSORS

The family of an intercessor invariably benefits from his or her commitment to prayer. Quite often the intercessor's life of prayer will help establish family direction and clarify God's purposes for each member of the family.

And, of course, prayer provides protection for the family. Anyone who has a praying mother or father, as I do, will attest to the fact that God moves when parents pray. The intercessor who appeals to God for the protection of his family is following Jesus' example (see John 17:15). Jesus prayed for His disciples, and He continues to pray for us today (see Rom. 8:34).

When an intercessor prays for her family, she is not only agreeing with God's plans for them, but she is releasing the ministry of angels on their behalf (see Dan. 10; Heb. 1:14).

SOCIETY BENEFITS FROM THE MINISTRY OF INTERCESSION

Intercessors are having a positive impact on our society. Cities across the nation are recording major drops in violent crime as more and more prayers for revival ascend as incense before the Lord.

According to many of our national spiritual leaders, there are signs of national revival on the horizon for the first time in 150 years. Historically, great harvests of souls have accompanied such outpourings of the Holy Spirit.

Hell's gates will not be able to withstand the power of a purified, unified, praying Church (see Matt. 16:18). Around the world we are seeing significant evidence that hell's gates are crumbling as a result of intercession. At last, Christ's prophecy and the Great Commission are on the verge of fulfillment!

HISTORY BELONGS TO THE INTERCESSOR

Where is all this leading? Simply put, as wickedness increases, God's activity on earth is increasing even more (see Rom. 5:20).

And God, for reasons known only to Him, has chosen throughout history to work in partnership with those that pray. As theologian Walter Wink said, "History belongs to the intercessor." If that is true, then the future, too, belongs to the intercessor!

THE GREAT COMMISSION

Growing numbers of Christians today are acquainted with the signs and are looking for the promise. God is setting the stage for a final great revival in the Church and a worldwide harvest of souls. The Great Commission was not just a great suggestion; it was a plan with a predictable end. God wastes no words and His plans never fail.

For years I lived with the expectation that evil would wax worse. I thought things might get so bad that God would rapture the Church to rescue us from a plan that went wrong. It's a sad theology. Why would Jesus give His Church a job, offer to help them complete it, then remove them because they proved unable to do so? That doesn't sound like an overcoming Church, does it? Satan would be thrilled to see the Church fail in its final effort. But She will not fail!

You can fully expect to see the Great Commission completed! Jesus promised it. John saw it. And now we are on the verge of its fulfillment. Dick Eastman gives us this counsel regarding the Great Commission:

> Frankly, the Church must become increasingly uncomfortable with the notion of merely reaching as many people as possible with the gospel before Jesus comes. We should settle for nothing less than "every creature," since anything less is outside the will of God (see 2 Pet. 3:9). We must employ every means and method to reach this goal, especially the simple, old-fashioned New Testament plan to go where people live.[1]

Anyone acquainted with world evangelism knows that we are seeing record numbers of people coming to Christ. With technology advancing at an astounding rate, many will benefit from the resulting explosion of knowledge, perhaps the lost being the greatest beneficiaries. Advances in communication systems alone will enable us to preach the gospel to every man, woman, boy and girl on earth!

There is also an historic level of unity in the Church today. Pastors and churches of various denominations are coming together around the person of Jesus Christ to complete the Great Commission.

The story goes that a traveling salesman was spending the night in a small town. Hearing a church bell ring, he inquired of the hotel clerk if there was a service that night.

"Yes," answered the clerk. "That is the Baptist bell ringing for the Methodist revival the Presbyterian evangelist is holding in the United Brethren Church."

OPEN THE FLOODGATES!

When I was a boy, I lived in the Rio Grande Valley of Texas on the Mexican border. There the residents have a rather unusual way of watering their lawns. Each person's lawn has a "built-up border" of dirt around it. In effect, the lawn is designed to contain water. The yard is connected via an underground pipeline to a reservoir. When a homeowner wants to water his lawn, he opens a valve a few inches below ground, and the yard is gradually flooded with life-giving water!

As life and health are returned to the sun-baked grass, the children can run and play in the water. I have fond memories of hot, summer, south Texas days when my brothers and I joined the other kids on the block to splash and play as our parents watered their lawns. It was a party!

When we pray for our neighborhoods, we open heaven's

valve, allowing God's blessings to flood our communities. Spiritual life and health are poured out from the reservoirs of heaven through the pipeline of prayer.

> I urge, then, first of all, that requests, prayers, intercession and thanksgiving be made for everyone—for kings and all those in authority, that we may live peaceful and quiet lives in all godliness and holiness (1 Tim. 2:1,2).

As life and health are returned to the sin-baked community, great joy and peace abound! Families are refreshed with the water of life. As priests, bridging the gap between the seen and the unseen through intercessory prayer, we are uniquely able to open the valve that releases God's blessings on our communities.

Before you close this book, I offer a prayer that it will provide fresh insight for you and your family and for the families of intercessors everywhere. From this insight may a restoration of relationships provide a foundation for revival in the United States and around the world!

A BELL IN THE NIGHT

The guided missile destroyer McCormick DDG-8, on which I served in the early 1960s, was a marvel of technology with all the bells and whistles. The most advanced U.S. Navy ship of its kind at that time, we were equipped with advanced radar and sonar systems and top secret ASROC (antisubmarine rocketry).

One night, well after midnight, I was standing watch atop the bridge in the South China Sea off the coast of Vietnam. The ship was clipping along on a moonless night through a pea-soup fog. The big ship slid at top speed through the bone-chilling cold night air. I was bundled from head to toe, binoculars in hand, fighting to stay awake. My thoughts drifted to my crewmates sound asleep in their warm bunks below deck. At the time, I could see little reason for me to be standing watch. After all, the McCormick was equipped with all the latest high-tech detection gadgetry.

Suddenly, I thought I heard a tiny, tinkling bell. A moment later, I was certain I was hearing a bell. It was so soft, I assumed it was off in the distance. Then I realized it was *very* close. I radioed a warning below for the captain to change direction. As the great ship slowly turned to starboard, there only a few yards ahead of us was a small Vietnamese junk. The frail wooden boat, lit with paper lanterns, had at least two full families aboard. As is their custom, they had their babies safely tied to the masts on leashes. My heart was gripped with fear for they seemed so helpless. Panic was written on their faces as their tiny, floating home slid safely past our bow. Weak-kneed, I breathed a sigh of relief.

Today's pastors and churches have a lot going for them. They have copiers, computers, fax machines, cell phones, web pages and all the latest gadgetry. They have highly trained, well-educated staffs. But nothing can replace a meaningful, interdependent partnership between themselves and committed intercessors who understand their watches and faithfully attend to them. There are lives hanging in the balance! Individuals, families and nations are at stake! It is time to take up the courage of Nehemiah and the tenacity of his people in order to see the Great Commission completed.

Many years ago on a lonely watch, I heard a faint bell and took action. I appealed to the captain and lives were saved. I can almost hear that bell today. This time you must join my appeal to the Captain of the heavenly host. Together we can see multitudes saved for eternity.

Note

1. Dick Eastman, *Beyond Imagination* (Grand Rapids: Chosen Books, 1997), p. 29.

Suggested Reading

Alves, Elizabeth. *Becoming a Prayer Warrior.* Ventura, CA: Regal Books, 1998.

Bickle, Mike. *Passion for Jesus.* Orlando: Creation House, 1993.

Billheimer, Paul E. *Destined for the Throne.* Ft. Washington, PA: Christian Literature Crusade, 1975.

Bonner, Mickey. *Brokenness, The Forgotten Factor.* Houston: Mickey Bonner Evangelistic Association, 1994.

———. *Hearing God's Voice from Within.* Houston: Mickey Bonner Evangelistic Assocation, 1998.

Bounds, E. M. *The Weapon of Prayer.* New Kensington, PA: Whitaker House, 1996.

Brown, Steve. *Approaching God.* Nashville: Moorings Publishing, 1996.

Bryant, David. *Stand in the Gap.* Ventura, CA: Regal Books, 1997.

Christenson, Evelyn. *A Time to Pray.* Eugene, OR: Harvest House, 1996.

Clinton, J. Robert. *The Making of a Leader.* Colorado Springs: NavPress, 1988.

Damazio, Frank. *The Making of a Leader.* Portland: Trilogy Productions, 1988.

———. *Seasons of Intercession.* Portland: BT Publishing, 1998.

Dawson, John. *Healing America's Wounds.* Ventura, CA: Regal Books, 1994.

———. *Taking Our Cities for God.* Lake Mary, FL: Creation House, 1990.

Deere, Jack. *Surprised by the Power of the Spirit.* Grand Rapids, MI: Zondervan Publishing House, 1993.

Eastman, Dick. *The Jericho Hour.* Altamonte Springs, FL: Creation House, 1994.

———. *Love on Its Knees.* Grand Rapids, MI: Fleming H. Revell Co., 1989.

———. *Beyond Imagination.* Grand Rapids, MI: Chosen Books, 1997.

Facius, Johannes. *Intercession.* Cambridge, Kent, England: Sovereign World Limited, 1993.

Floyd, Ronnie. *The Power of Prayer and Fasting.* Nashville: Broadman & Holman, 1997.

Frangipane, Francis. *The House of the Lord.* Lake Mary, FL: Creation House, 1991.

Ginter, Dian. *Power House.* Nashville: Broadman & Holman, 1994.

Goll, Jim. *The Lost Art of Intercession.* Shippensburg, PA: Destiny Image Publishers, 1997.

Grubb, Norman. *Rees Howells, Intercessor.* Fort Washington, PA: Christian Literature Crusade, 1962.

Guyon, Jeanne. *Experiencing the Depths of Jesus Christ.* Gardiner, ME: Christian Books, 1981.

Hansen, Jane. *The Journey of a Woman.* Ventura, CA: Regal Books, 1998.

———. *Fashioned for Intimacy.* Ventura, CA: Regal Books, 1997.

Jacobs, Cindy. *Possessing the Gates of the Enemy.* Grand Rapids, MI: Chosen Books, 1991.

———. *The Voice of God.* Ventura, CA: Regal Books, 1995.

Kinnamen, Gary. *Overcoming the Dominion of Darkness.* Grand Rapids, MI: Chosen Books, 1990.

Lea, Larry. *Releasing the Prayer Anointing.* Nashville: Thomas Nelson Publishers, 1996.

Murray, Andrew. *The Ministry of Intercession.* New Kensington, PA: Whitaker House, 1982.

Nee, Watchman. *Spiritual Authority.* Richmond, VA: Christian Fellowship Publisher, 1972.

———. *The Release of the Spirit.* Cloverdale, IN: Sure Foundation Publishers, 1965.

Otis Jr., George. *The Last of the Giants.* Grand Rapids, MI: Chosen Books, 1991.

———. *The Twilight Labyrinth.* Grand Rapids, MI: Chosen Books, 1998.

Prime, Samuel, *The Power of Prayer.* Carlisle, PA: The Banner of Truth, 1991.

Prince, Derek. *Shaping History through Prayer and Fasting.* Ft. Lauderdale, FL: Derek Prince Ministries, 1973.

Shanklin, Steven L. *The Book of Prayers.* New York: St. Martin's Press, 1998.

Sheets, Dutch. *Intercessory Prayer.* Ventura, CA: Regal Books, 1997.

Sherrer, Quin, and Garlock, Ruthanne. *A Woman's Guide to Breaking Bondages.* Ann Arbor, MI: Servant Publications, 1994.

———. *The Spiritual Warrior's Prayer Guide.* Ann Arbor, MI: Servant Publications, 1992.

Silvoso, Ed. *That None Should Perish.* Ventura, CA: Regal Books, 1994.

Sjöberg, Kjell. *Winning the Prayer War.* Ventura, CA: Renew Books, 1991.

Smith, Alice. *Beyond the Veil.* Ventura, CA: Regal Books, 1997.

Smith, Rolland C. *The Watchmen Ministry.* St. Louis: Mission Omega Publishing, 1993.

Wagner, C. Peter. *Breaking Strongholds in Your City.* Ventura, CA: Regal Books, 1993.

———. *Churches That Pray.* Ventura, CA: Regal Books, 1993.

———. *Confronting the Powers.* Ventura, CA: Regal Books, 1996.

———. *Engaging the Enemy.* Ventura, CA: Regal Books, 1991.

———. *Lighting the World.* Ventura, CA: Regal Books, 1995.

———. *Prayer Shield.* Ventura, CA: Regal Books, 1992.

———. *Warfare Prayer.* Ventura, CA: Regal Books, 1992.

———. *Your Spiritual Gifts Can Help Your Church Grow.* Ventura, CA: Regal Books, 1979; revised edition, 1994.

White, Tom. *Breaking Strongholds.* Ann Arbor, MI: Servant Publications, 1993.

Conferences, Seminars, Retreats

Eddie and Alice Smith, in association with the *U.S. PRAYER TRACK*, travel worldwide teaching on various themes related to revival and spiritual awakening.

Contact Greg Greenwood at our office if you would like additional information about hosting a conference with the Smiths in your church or city. Eddie and Alice are available to teach, together or separately. Their topics include: prayer, intercession, deliverance, worship, spiritual warfare, spiritual mapping, Etc. Call: 1-713-466-4009, Ext. 308.

& PrayerNet Newsletter

Alice smith is senior editor of this biweekly, innovative, up-to-the-minute cyberspace publication. Best of all, its **FREE**! Join thousands worldwide who receive PrayerNet! Send a two-word message "subscribe prayernet" to 75711.2501@CompuServe.com to activate your subscription today. Also, check out our internet web page at http://www.usprayertrack.org.

PrayUSA!

You are invited to join millions of other Christians in 40-days of prayer and fasting for revival and spiritual awakening in the United States each spring.

For more information about *PrayUSA!*, contact: *U.S. PRAYER TRACK*, 7710-T Cherry Park Drive, Suite 224, Houston, TX 77095

Pastors and churches are gathering regularly across the United States to pray for revival, spiritual awakening and an evangelistic harvest! Concerts of prayer, pastors' prayer summits, prayerwalking, neighborhood houses of prayer, prayer and fasting, spiritual warfare prayer, student prayer at school, and marketplace prayer are just a few of the creative ways Christians are becoming involved in prayer. Churches in record numbers are developing prayer ministries, hiring staff prayer coordinators and building prayer rooms. Today most evangelical denominations have their own national prayer leaders.

Movements unlike organizations, are not led; they are facilitated. The *U.S. PRAYER TRACK* is one of the primary facilitators for the U.S. prayer movement.

U.S. PRAYER TRACK

The primary purpose of the *U.S. PRAYER TRACK* is to mobilize prayer for revival and spiritual awakening in the United States by identifying and network existing prayer ministries.

In addition, the *U.S. PRAYER TRACK* exists to serve other prayer ministries by offering consultation, publication of instructional and inspirational prayer-related materials and teaching on subjects related to prayer and spiritual warfare.

7710-T Cherry Park Drive, Suite 224 • Houston, TX 77095
Phone: (713) 466-4009 • Fax: (713) 466-5633
Email: 75711.2501@CompuServe. com
Website: www.usprayertrack.org

MDIA TUTOR

410-296 00 10

1 JOHN 3:16   PEACE

13